BIG RED
SONGBOOK

GW00457096

Pluto Press

The Big Red Songbook
This enlarged edition first published 1981 by Pluto Press Limited,
Unit 10 Spencer Court, 7 Chalcot Road, London NW1 8LH

This collection first published 1977
by Pluto Press

Copyright © Pluto Press 1977, 1981
ISBN 0 86104 356 1

Designed by Pearce Marchbank

Printed in Great Britain by Mayhew McCrimmon Printers Ltd

BIG RED SONGBOOK

Compiled by Mal Collins, Dave Harker
and Geoff White

AS SOON AS THIS PUB CLOSES
Alex Glasgow 50/106

THE BALLAD OF ACCOUNTING
Ewan MacColl 18/80

THE BALLAD OF JOHN MACLEAN
Matt McGinn 22/115

BANDIERA ROSSA
Anon. 13/77

BATTLE HYMN OF THE NEW SOCIALIST PARTY
Leon Rosselson 44/101

THE BLACKLEG MINER
Anon. 52/109

BREAD AND ROSES
James Oppenheim/Caroline Kohslat 38/97

BROWNED OFF
Ewan MacColl 24/84

CASEY JONES
Joe Hill 71/126

CHEMICAL WORKERS
Ron Angel 43/100

CLOSE THE COAL-HOUSE DOOR
Alex Glasgow 32/94

THE DURHAM STRIKE
Tommy Armstrong 70/123

THE FIRST TIME EVER I SAW YOUR FACE
Ewan MacColl 42/99

THE FOUR LOOM WEAVER
Anon. 64/118

GO DOWN YOU MURDERERS

Ewan MacColl 40/98

HALLELUJAH I'M A BUM

Harry McClintock 55/111

I'M GONNA BE AN ENGINEER

Peggy Seeger 46/102

THE INTERNATIONAL

Eugene Pottier/Pierre Degeyter 10/74

JOIN THE BRITISH ARMY

Anon. 48/104

McALPINE'S FUSILIERS

Dominic Behan 49/107

THE MAN THAT WATERS THE WORKERS' BEER

Paddy Ryan 58/113

MOTOR TRADE WORKERS

Don Perrygrove 28/92

MRS McGRATH

Anon. 59/82

OAKEY STRIKE EVICTIONS

Tommy Armstrong 62/114

THE OLD MAN'S SONG

Ian Campbell 30/81

PALACES OF GOLD

Leon Rosselson 27/88

THE PEAT-BOG SOLDIERS

Anon. 56/112

THE PEELERS AND THE GOAT

Anon. 53/110

THE POUND-A-WEEK RISE

Ed Pickford 66/91

THE PREACHER AND THE SLAVE
Joe Hill 54/108

THE RED FLAG
Jim Connell 12/76

THE SOCIALIST A.B.C.
Alex Glasgow 19/120

SOLIDARITY FOREVER
Ralph Chaplin 72/127

STANDING AT THE DOOR
Alex Glasgow 36/96

STRANGE FRUIT
Lewis Allan 20/90

THREE NIGHTS AND A SUNDAY DOUBLE-TIME
Matt McGinn 61/124

TURNING THE CLOCK BACK
Alex Glasgow 31/116

UNDERGROUND ARISTOCRATS
Pat Cooksey 68/122

UNION MAID
Woody Guthrie 60/86

VIGILANTE MAN
Woody Guthrie 34/95

VIVA LA QUINCE BRIGADA
Anon. 14/78

WILLIAM BROWN
Arthur Hagg 26/85

THE WORLD TURNED UPSIDE DOWN
Leon Rosselson 16/79

Acknowledgements

As Soon As This Pub Closes reproduced with permission of
Alex Glasgow

The Ballad Of Accounting reproduced with permission of
Ewan MacColl and Harmony Music Ltd, The Essex Music Group,
19-20 Poland Street, London W1V 3DD

*The Ballad Of John Maclean and Three Nights And A Sunday
Double Time* Copyright © 1967 Heathside Music Ltd,
86 Marylebone High Street, London W1M 4AY
and reproduced with permission

Battle Hymn Of The New Socialist Party Copyright © 1966
Harmony Music Ltd, The Essex Music Group, 19-20 Poland Street,
London W1V 3DD and reproduced with permission

Close The Coal-house Door reproduced with permission of
Robbins Music Corp. Ltd, 138-40 Charing Cross Road,
London WC2H 0LD

The First Time Ever I Saw Your Face reproduced with permission
of Ewan MacColl and Harmony Music Ltd, The Essex Music Group,
19-20 Poland Street, London W1V 3DD

Go Down You Murderers reproduced with permission of
Ewan MacColl and Harmony Music Ltd, The Essex Music Group,
19-20 Poland Street, London W1V 3DD

I'm Gonna Be An Engineer reproduced with permission of
Peggy Seeger and Harmony Music Ltd, The Essex Music Group,
19-20 Poland Street, London W1V 3DD

The Man Who Waters The Workers' Beer reproduced with
permission of the Workers Music Association,
236 Westbourne Park Road, London W11 1EL

The Old Man's Song Copyright © 1966 Heathside Music Ltd,
86 Marylebone High Street, London W1M 4AY
and reproduced with permission

Palaces Of Gold Copyright © 1967 Harmony Music Ltd,
The Essex Music Group, 19-20 Poland Street, London W1V 3DD
and reproduced with permission

The Pound-A-Week Rise reproduced with permission of
Ed Pickford

Strange Fruit reproduced with permission of Planetary-Nom
(London) Ltd, 143 Charing Cross Road, London WC2H 0EE

The Socialist ABC reproduced with permission of Alex Glasgow

Standing At The Door reproduced with permission of
Robbins Music Corp. Ltd, 138-40 Charing Cross Road,
London WC2H 0LD

Turning The Clock Back reproduced with permission of
Alex Glasgow

Underground Aristocrats reproduced with permission of
Pat Cooksey

Union Maid reproduced with permission of
Tro-Essex Music Ltd, The Essex Music Group,
19-20 Poland Street, London W1V 3DD

Vigilante Man reproduced with permission of
Tro-Essex Music Ltd, The Essex Music Group,
19-20 Poland Street, London W1V 3DD

The World Turned Upside Down Copyright © 1974
Leon Rosselson and reproduced with permission

Chemical Workers reproduced with permission
of Ron Angel

McAlpine's Fusiliers reproduced with permission
of Dominic Behan

Motor Trade Workers reproduced with permission of
Don Perrygrove

Photograph and illustration credits
Camera Press: pages 12, 14, 40, 41, 50
Miles Archives: page 10
Oscar Zarate: page 16
Patrick Ward: page 28
Sport and General: page 44
Bob Golden: page 37

Compilers' note

We hope to have put together a collection of
songs suitable for the widest range of singers and
audiences. We have included some of the standard
socialist anthems but hope also to have given a fair
sample of songs from the labour movement in
Britain and, to a lesser extent, Europe and
North America. We have given the earliest text
available and, where possible, the tune specified
by the writer. We have been refused
permission, we regret, for a few songs we had
originally selected.
We'd like to thank Mike Kidron, Alex Glasgow,
Ed Pickford, Pat Cooksey, Matt McGinn,
David Craig, Colin Barker, Ewan MacColl,
Peggy Seeger, Leon Rosselson, Hamish Henderson,
Ian Winship and the many people who have
encouraged us through their enthusiasm
for this project.

Written by Eugene Pottier, a woodworker from Lille, in
1871, after the Paris Commune was ruthlessly suppressed.
It was set to music by Degeyter in 1888.
   The American and English versions are both given
here. *The International* was the official anthem of the
Soviet Union until 1943 when it was dropped in favour of
In Praise of Great Russia.

Eugene Pottier

THE INTERNATIONAL

Arise, ye pris'ners of starvation!
Arise, ye wretched of the earth,
For justice thunders condemnation,
A better world's in birth.
No more tradition's chain shall bind us,
Arise, ye slaves; No more in thrall!
The earth shall rise on new foundations,
We have been naught, we shall be all.
Chorus;
 'Tis the final conflict,
 Let each stand in his place,
 The international party
 Shall be the human race.

We want no condescending saviours,
To rule us from a judgment hall;
We workers ask not for their favors,
Let us consult for all.
To make the thief disgorge his boot,
To free the spirit from its cell,
We must ourselves decide our duty,
We must decide and do it well.

The law oppresses us and tricks us.
Taxation drains the victim's blood;
The rich are free from obligations,
The laws the poor delude.
Too long we've languished in subjection,
Equality has other laws:
'No right,' says she, 'without their duties,
No claim on equals without cause.'

Behold them seated in their glory,
The kings of mine and rail and soil!
What have you read in all their story,
But how they plundered toil?
Fruits of the people's toil are buried
In the strong coffers of a few;
In voting for their restitution,
The men will only ask their due.

Toilers from shops and fields united,
The party we of all who work;
The earth belongs to us, the people,
No room here for the shirk!
How many on our flesh have fattened!
But if the noisome birds of prey
Shall vanish from the sky some morning,
The blessed sunlight still will stay.

(English version)

Arise ye starvelings from your slumbers;
Arise ye criminals of want.
For Reason in revolt now thunders,
And at last ends the age of cant.
Now away with all your superstitions,
Servile masses arise! Arise!
We'll change forthwith the old conditions,
And spurn the dust to win the prize.
Chorus;
 Then comrades come rally,
 And the last fight let us face.
 The International
 Unites the human race.
 (Repeat)

We peasants, artisans and others;
Enrolled among the sons of toil.
Let's claim the earth henceforth for brothers.
Drive the indolent from the soil.
On our flesh too long has fed the raven;
We've too long been the vulture's prey.
But now, farewell the spirit craven,
The dawn brings in a brighter day.
Chorus;

No saviour from on high delivers;
No trust have we in prince or peer.
Our own right hand the chains must shiver;
Chains of hatred, of greed and fear.
Ere the thieves will out with their booty
And to all give a happier lot.
Each at his forge must do his duty
And strike the iron while it's hot.
Chorus;

Inspired by the 1889 London dock strike and set to an
old Jacobite tune 'The White Cockade'.
It wasn't until years later that the words were put to
the traditional German tune, *Tannenbaum*.

Jim Connell, an Irishman, described himself as a
one time 'sheep farmer, dock labourer, navvy, railway-
man, draper, lawyer (of a sort) and all time poacher'.
He claimed to have written the song on a fifteen minute
train journey between Charing Cross and New Cross
stations. It was first published in the Christmas edition
of *Justice*, the paper of the Social Democratic
Federation, in 1889.

Jim Connell

THE RED FLAG

The people's flag is deepest red,
It shrouded oft our martyred dead.
And ere their limbs grew stiff and cold,
Their hearts' blood dyed to every fold.
Chorus;

    Then raise the scarlet standard high;
    Beneath its folds we'll live and die.
    Though cowards flinch and traitors sneer,
    We'll keep the red flag flying here.

Look 'round, the Frenchman loves its blaze,
The sturdy German chants its praise;
In Moscow's vaults its hymns are sung,
Chicago swells the surging throng.
Chorus;

It waved above our infant might
When all ahead seemed dark as night;
It witnessed many a deed and vow,
We must not change its colour now.
Chorus;

It well recalls the triumphs past;
It gives the hope of peace at last —
The banner bright, the symbol plain
Of human right and human gain.
Chorus;

It suits today the meek and base,
Whose minds are fixed on pelf and place,
To cringe beneath the rich man's frown,
And haul that sacred emblem down.
Chorus;

With heads uncovered swear we all
To bare it onward till we fall.
Come dungeons dark or gallows grim,
This song shall be our parting hymn.
Chorus;

Bandiera Rossa is the Italian equivalent of *The Red Flag*
— a theme song in both Communist and Socialist Party
rallies.

BANDIERA ROSSA

Avanti popolo, a la rescossa;
Bandiera rossa, bandiera rossa.
Avanti popolo, a la rescossa;
Bandiera rossa trionferà.
  Bandiera rossa trionferà
  Bandiera rossa trionferà
  Bandiera rossa trionferà.
  Evviva comunismo e liberta.

Arise you workers, fling to the breezes
The scarlet banner, the scarlet banner.
Arise you workers, fling to the breezes
The scarlet banner, triumphantly.
  Wave scarlet banners triumphantly
  Wave scarlet banners triumphantly
  Wave scarlet banners triumphantly.
  For communism and liberty.

Arise you workers, your chains of slavery
Will vanish under the scarlet banner.
Come rally round it, come show your bravery;
The scarlet banner, triumphantly.
  Wave scarlet banners triumphantly
  Wave scarlet banners triumphantly
  Wave scarlet banners triumphantly.
  For communism and liberty.

The battle song of the International Brigade during the Spanish Civil War.

The song can be heard on the Campbells' *Songs of Protest* EP (Topic Records, TOP 82).

VIVA LA QUINCE BRIGADA

Viva la Quince Brigada,
Rhum-ba-la, rhum-ba-la, rhum-ba-la.
Viva la Quince Brigada,
Rhum-ba-la, rhum-ba-la, rhum-ba-la.
Que se-ha cubierta de gloria,
Ay Manuela, ay Manuela.

Luchamos contra los Morros,
Rhum-ba-la, rhum-ba-la, rhum-ba-la.
Mercenairos y fascistas,
Rhum-ba-la, rhum-ba-la, rhum-ba-la.

Soloex nuestro deseo,
Rhum-ba-la, rhum-ba-la, rhum-ba-la.
Acabar con el fascismo,
Rhum-ba-la, rhum-ba-la, rhum-ba-la.

En el frente de Jarama,
Rhum-ba-la, rhum-ba-la, rhum-ba-la.
No tenemos ni aviones,
Rhum-ba-la, rhum-ba-la, rhum-ba-la.
Ni tankes, ni canones,
Ay Manuela, ay Manuela.

Ya Salimos de Espana,
Rhum-ba-la, rhum-ba-la, rhum-ba-la.
Por Luchar en otras frontes,
Rhum-ba-la, rhum-ba-la, rhum-ba-la.

Viva the fifteenth brigade!
Rhum-ba-la, rhum-ba-la, rhum-ba-la.
Viva the fifteenth brigade!
Rhum-ba-la, rhum-ba-la, rhum-ba-la.
Which has covered itself in glory.
Alas Manuela, alas Manuela.

We struggle against the Moors,
Rhum-ba-la, rhum-ba-la, rhum-ba-la.
Mercenaries and fascists,
Rhum-ba-la, rhum-ba-la, rhum-ba-la.

Our only wish,
Rhum-ba-la, rhum-ba-la, rhum-ba-la.
To put an end to fascism,
Rhum-ba-la, rhum-ba-la, rhum-ba-la.

On the Jarama Front,
Rhum-ba-la, rhum-ba-la, rhum-ba-la.
We have no aeroplanes,
Rhum-ba-la, rhum-ba-la, rhum-ba-la.
Nor tanks, nor guns,
Alas Manuela, alas Manuela.

Already we are leaving Spain,
Rhum-ba-la, rhum-ba-la, rhum-ba-la.
To fight on other fronts,
Rhum-ba-la, rhum-ba-la, rhum-ba-la.

translated by Geoff White.

In March 1649, the Diggers, a group of early communists, occupied St George's Hill near Walton-on-Thames and proclaimed it a classless society. After a year of heroic struggle and near starvation they were finally forced off the land by local landed interests and Fairfax's troops.

'This particular propriety of mine and thine hath brought in all misery upon the people. For, first it hath occasioned people to steal from one another. Secondly, it hath made laws to hang people that did steal.' Gerrard Winstanley.

This song can be heard on Leon Rosselson's *That's Not The Way It's Got To Be* LP (Acorn Records, CF 251). For more on Leon Rosselson see page 44.

Leon Rosselson

THE WORLD TURNED UPSIDE DOWN

In sixteen forty nine to St George's Hill
A ragged band they called the Diggers came to show the people's will.
They defied the landlords, they defied the laws,
They were the dispossessed re-claiming what was theirs.

We come in peace, they said, to dig and sow.
We come to work the land in common and
   to make the waste ground grow
This earth divided, we will make whole
So it will be a common treasury for all.

The sin of property we do disdain.
No man has any right to buy and
   sell the earth for private gain.
By theft and murder they took the land
Now everywhere the walls spring up
   at their command.

They make the laws to chain us well.
The clergy dazzle us with heaven or they damn us into hell.
We will not worship the God they serve
The God of greed who feeds the rich while poor men starve.

We work, we eat together, we need no swords.
We will not bow to masters or pay rent to the lords.
We are free men, though we are poor,
You Diggers all stand up for Glory, stand up now.

From the men of property the orders came.
They sent the hired men and troopers to wipe
   out the Diggers' claim.
Tear down their cottages, destroy their corn.
They were dispersed — only the vision lingers on.

You poor take courage, you rich take care.
This earth was made a common treasury
   for everyone to share;
All things in common, all people one
We come in peace — the orders came to cut them down.

Born Jimmy Miller, in 1915, MacColl spent most of his childhood in Salford, Lancashire. In 1945 he and Joan Littlewood formed the Theatre Workshop in London. In the 1950s he was closely involved with the embryo folk club movement, and, in 1956, he joined Charles Parker and Peggy Seeger in producing the first radio ballad, *The Ballad of John Axon.* A regular contributor to radio and TV, MacColl has made upwards of sixty LPs on his own and many more with other singers, notably Peggy Seeger.

Many of MacColl's earlier songs are to be found in the *Ewan MacColl/Peggy Seeger Songbook* (New York, Oak, 1963), while more recent ones are included in the *New City Songsters* series published by MacColl and Seeger from 35, Stanley Avenue, Beckenham, Kent. *The Ballad of Accounting* can be heard on their *Folkways Record of Contemporary Songs* (Folkways Records, New York 1973, FW 8736).

Ewan MacColl

THE BALLAD OF ACCOUNTING

In the morning we built the city
In the afternoon walked through its streets
Evening saw us leaving;
We wandered through our days as if they would never end,
All of us imagined we had endless time to spend.
We hardly saw the crossroads and small attention gave,
To landmarks on the journey from the cradle to the grave.
CRADLE TO THE GRAVE, CRADLE TO THE GRAVE.

Did you learn to dream in the morning?
Abandon dreams in the afternoon?
Wait without hope in the evening?
Did you stand there in the traces and let 'em feed you lies?
Did you trail along behind 'em wearing blinkers on your eyes?
Did you kiss the foot that kicked you? Did you thank 'em for their scorn?
Did you ask for their forgiveness for the act of being born?
ACT OF BEING BORN, ACT OF BEING BORN?

Did you alter the face of the city?
Make any change in the world you found?
Or did you observe all the warnings?
Did you read the trespass notices, did you keep off the grass?
Did you shuffle off the pavement just to let your betters pass?
Did you learn to keep your mouth shut, were you seen and never heard?
Did you learn to be obedient and jump to at a   word?
AND JUMP TO AT A WORD, JUMP TO AT A WORD?

Did you ever demand any answers,
The who and the what and the reason why?
Did you ever question the set up?
Did you stand aside and let 'em choose while you took second best?
Did you let 'em skim the cream off and then give to you the rest?
Did you settle for the shoddy and did you think it right?
To let 'em rob you right and left and never make a fight?
NEVER MAKE A FIGHT, NEVER MAKE A FIGHT?

What did you learn in the morning?
How much did you know in the afternoon?
Were you content in the evening?
Did they teach you how to question when you were at school?
Did the factory help you grow, were you the maker or the tool?
Did the place where you were living enrich your life, and then —
Did you reach some understanding of all your fellow men?
ALL YOUR FELLOW MEN, ALL YOUR FELLOW MEN?

From the play *Close the Coalhouse Door*. The original can be heard on *Songs of Alex Glasgow* LP (Mawson and Wareham Music, 1973, MWM 1006). For more on Alex Glasgow see page 51.

Alex Glasgow

THE SOCIALIST A.B.C.

When that I was and a little tiny boy,
Me daddy said to me,
'The time has come, me bonny, bonny bairn
To learn your ABC.'
Now Daddy was a Lodge Chairman
In the coalfields of the Tyne,
And that ABC was different
From the Enid Blyton kind.
He sang;
A is for Alienation that made me the man that I am and B's for the Boss,
who's a bastard, a bourgeois who don't give a damn.
C is for Capitalism, the boss's reactionary creed and D's for Dictatorship,
laddie, but the best proletarian breed.
E is for Exploitation, that the workers have suffered so long;
and F is for old Ludwig Feuerbach, the first one to see it was wrong,
G is for all Gerrymanderers, like Lord Muck and Sir Whatsisname,
and H is the Hell that they'll go to, when the workers have kindled the flame.
I is for Imperialism, and America's kind is the worst,
and J is for sweet Jingoism, that the Tories all think of first.
K is for good old Keir Hardie, who fought out the working class fight
and L is for Vladimir Lenin, who showed him the Left was all right.
M is of course for Karl Marx, the daddy and the mammy of them all,
and N is for Nationalisation, without it we'd crumble and fall.
O is for Overproduction that capitalist economy brings,
and P is for all Private Property, the greatest of all of the sins.
Q is for the Quid pro quo, that we'll deal out so well and so soon,
when R for Revolution is shouted and the Red Flag becomes the top tune.
S is for sad Stalinism, that gave us all such a bad name,
and T is for Trotsky the hero, who had to take all of the blame.
U's for the Union of workers, the Union will stand to the end,
and V is for Vodka, yes, Vodka, the one drink that don't bring the bends.
W is for all Willing workers, and that's where the memory fades,
for X, Y and Z, me dear daddy said, will be written on the street barricades.

But now that I'm not a little tiny boy,
Me daddy says to me,
'Please try to forget the things I said,
Especially the ABC.'
For Daddy's no longer a Union man,
And he's had to change his plea.
His alphabet is different now;
Since they made him a Labour MP.

This song was first recorded by jazz singer Billie Holiday,
with the Teddy Wilson band in December 1939, when she
was at the height of her creative powers. By taking the theme
out of the good-humoured, stoical confines of the blues, she
spoke for a newer generation of urban black performers. It
was a courageous thing to do at a time when jazz was
becoming safe for white audiences and every middle class
socialite wanted to dance to Ellington or Count Basie.

The tragic theme of *Strange Fruit*, captured in that first
recording, was to be underscored by the pathos of Billie
Holiday's own life. Her body raked by drugs and her talent
crippled, she died a lonely death in New York in 1959, at the
age of 44. The police waited at her bedside to arrest her for
narcotics offences. *Strange Fruit* can be heard on *Billie
Holiday: The Commodore Days* (AHC 184).

Lewis Allan

STRANGE FRUIT

Southern trees bear a strange fruit;
Blood on the leaves, blood at the root.
Black body swinging in the Southern breeze,
Strange fruit hanging from the poplar trees.
Oh——————Oh——————
Pastoral scenes of the gallant South,
The bulging eyes and the twisted mouth.
Scent of magnolia sweet and fresh,
And the sudden smell of burning flesh.
Here is a fruit for the crows to pluck;
For the rain to gather, for the wind to suck.
For the sun to rot, for the trees to drop
Oh——————Here is a strange and bitter crop.
Oh——————Here is a strange and bitter crop.

This describes the welcome given to the famous Scottish marxist on his release from prison in 1917. Maclean had been imprisoned for campaigning against the war; he was soon to return to jail for his activities around the Red Clyde shop stewards' struggles of 1918-19.

Matt McGinn was born in Glasgow in 1928, one of nine children. He went to an approved school, followed in his father's footsteps as an unskilled labourer and then, after a trade union scholarship to Ruskin College, Oxford, became a teacher and later one of Scotland's first adventure playground leaders. He sang more or less professionally from 1962. He died tragically in January 1977, two weeks before his forty-ninth birthday.

This song can be heard on *Matt McGinn Again* (Transatlantic Records, 1967, XTRA 1057). More of Matt's songs can be found in print in *Scottish Songs Today* (London, Harmony Music, 1964).

Matt McGinn

THE BALLAD OF JOHN MACLEAN

Tell me where you gan lad,
And who yer gan to meet.
I'm heading for the station
That's in Macadam Street.
I'll join two hundred thousand
That's there to meet the train.
That's bringing back to Glasgow
Our own dear John Maclean.
Chorus;

    Dominay, Dominay;[1]
    There was none like John Maclean,
    The fighting Dominay.

Tell me where's he been lad?
Why has he been there?
They've had him in the prison
For preaching in the Square.
Johnny held a finger
At all the ills he saw.
He was right side o' the people
And wrong side o' the law.
Chorus;

1. teacher

Johnny was a teacher
In one of Glasgow's schools.
The golden law was silence,
But Johnny broke the rules.
For a world of social justice
Young Johnny could ne wait;
He took his chalk and easel
To the men at the shipyard gate.
Chorus;

The leaders of the nation
Make money hand o'er fist;
By grinding down the people
With the fiddle and the twist.
Aided and abetted
By preacher and the press.
John called for Revolution,
And he called for nothing less.
Chorus;

The bosses and the judges
United as one man.
For Johnny was a menace
To the '14-'18 plan.
They wanted men for slaughter
On the fields of Armentières;
John called upon the people
To smash the profiteers.
Chorus;

They brought him to the courtroom
In Edinburgh town.
But still he did not cower,
He firmly held his ground
And stoutly he defended
His every word and deed;
Five years it was the sentence
In the jail of Peterheid.
Chorus;

Seven months he lingered
In prison misery.
The people roused in fury
In Glasgow and Dundee.
Lloyd George and all his cronies
Were shaken to the core.
The prison gates were open
And Johnny's free once more.
Chorus;

Written during the 'phoney war' period of 1940 and first sung at Catterick Camp, from where it allegedly 'swept the British Army like wildfire'. North Western Command responded by organising a song-writing competition to elicit a politically more acceptable alternative. They failed.
  Browned Off can be heard on *Bundook Ballads* (Topic Records, 1965, 12T130).

Ewan MacColl

BROWNED OFF

I used to be a civvy, chum, as decent as can be;
I used to think a working lad had a man's right to be free
And then one day they made a lousy soldier out of me
And told me I had got to save democracy.
Chorus;
    Oh I was browned off, browned off, browned off as can be.
    Browned off, browned off, an easy mark that's me.
    But when this war is over, and again I'm free,
    There'll be no more trips around the world for me.

24

They stuck me in a convict's suit, they made me cut me hair.
They took me civvy shoes away, they gave me another pair.
Instead of grub they gave me slush and plenty of fresh air
And this was all to help to save democracy.
Chorus;

Now every day I'm on parade long before the dawn.
And every day I curse the day that I was born.
For I am just a browned off soldier, anyone can see;
They browned me off to help to save democracy.
Chorus;

The colonel kicks the major, then the major has to go,
He kicks the poor old captain who then kicks the NCO.
And as the kicks get harder the poor private, you can see,
Gets kicked to ruddy hell to save democracy.
Chorus;

First published in the 1927 edition of the *ILP Songbook*.
The versions of Verses 4 and 6 are by Bill Keable as is the
additional verse and chorus to end the song.

Arthur Hagg

WILLIAM BROWN

A nice young man was William Brown,
He worked for a wage in a Yorkshire town;
He turned a wheel from left to right,
From eight at morning till six at night.
Chorus;
    Now keep that wheel a turning
    Keep that wheel a turning
    Keep that wheel a turning
    And do a little more each day.

The boss one day to William came.
'Look here', he said, 'Young what's your name.
We're far from pleased with what you do;
So hurry that wheel or out you go!'
    Now keep that wheel a turning
    Keep that wheel a turning
    Keep that wheel a turning
    And do a little more each day.

So William turned and he made her run
Three times round in the place of one.
He turned so hard he was quickly made
The Lord High Turner of his trade.
    Now keep that wheel a turning
    Keep that wheel a turning
    Keep that wheel a turning
    And do a little more each day.

His fame spread wide o'er hill and dale.
His face appeared in the Daily Mail.
Cheap coach trips were organised
All to gaze at the lad's blue eyes.
    Now keep that wheel a turning
    Keep that wheel a turning
    Keep that wheel a turning
    And do a little more each day.

Still William turned with a saintly smile;
The goods he made grew such a pile.
They filled his room and the room next door
And overflowed to the basement floor.
    Now keep that wheel a turning
    Keep that wheel a turning
    Keep that wheel a turning
    And do a little more each day.

But sad the sequel now to tell;
With profits raised the boss could sell
To take-over group from London town.
The first redundant case was Brown!
Chorus;
    Now he's in the queue a' waiting,
    He's in the queue a' waiting,
    He's in the queue a' waiting,
    And he gets a little thinner each day.

Now workers don't be such a clown,
But take a tip from William Brown.
If you work too hard you'll surely be
Wiser but poorer same as he.
Chorus;
    For he's in the queue a' waiting,
    He's in the queue a' waiting,
    He's in the queue a' waiting
    And he gets a little thinner each day.

Published in *Look Here: Songs by Leon Rosselson* and
recorded on *Palaces of Gold* LP (Acorn Records, 1975,
CF 249). Also sung well by Roy Bailey on *Roy Bailey* LP
(Leader Sound, 1971, Trailer LER 3021).

Leon Rosselson

PALACES OF GOLD

If the sons of company directors,
And judges' private daughters,
Had to go to school in a slum school,
Dumped by some joker in a damp back alley,
Had to herd into classrooms cramped with worry,
With a view onto slag heaps and stagnant pools,
Had to file through corridors grey with age,
And play in a crack-pot concrete cage.

> Buttons would be pressed,
> Rules would be broken.
> Strings would be pulled
> And magic words spoken.
> Invisible fingers would mould
> Palaces of gold.

If prime ministers and advertising executives,
Royal personages and bank managers' wives
Had to live out their lives in dank rooms,
Blinded by smoke and the foul air of sewers.
Rot on the walls and rats in the cellars,
In rows of dumb houses like mouldering tombs.
Had to bring up their children and watch them grow
In a wasteland of dead streets where nothing will grow.

> Buttons would be pressed,
> Rules would be broken.
> Strings would be pulled
> And magic words spoken
> Invisible fingers would mould
> Palaces of gold.

I'm not suggesting any sort of plot,
Everyone knows there's not,
But you unborn millions might like to be warned
That if you don't want to be buried alive by slagheaps,
Pitfalls and damp walls and rat traps and dead streets,
Arrange to be democratically born
The son of a company director
Or a judge's private daughter.

> Buttons would be pressed,
> Rules would be broken.
> Strings would be pulled
> And magic words spoken.
> Invisible fingers would mould
> Palaces of gold.

Don Perrygrove worked in the car industry for 22 years and he is now at Cambridge University. He wrote the song in 1970 when he was still a carworker. It can be heard on *The Wide Midlands* (Topic Records, 12TS210). Don can be found at 367 Brownfield Road, Shard End, Birmingham.

Don Perrygrove

MOTOR TRADE WORKERS

Oh we are two motor trade workers;
We're labelled as loafers and shirkers.
We're crippling the country the newspapers say,
With too low an output and far too much pay.
Far too much pay,
Far too much pay,
With too low an output and far too much pay.

Each morning we leave around seven,
And drive to our mechanised heaven.
We make cans of tea, have a lark and a crack,
Till the half-seven bell rings and off goes the track.
Off goes the track,
Off goes the track,
Till the half-seven bell rings and off goes the track.

Our track is a steel over-seer,
We pray he'll break down, but no fe-ar.
For his vital organs are switches and nobs;
And he has us poor working lads sweating great cobs,
Sweating great cobs,
Sweating great cobs,
And he has us poor working lads sweating great cobs.

We're pressing and turning and milling,
We're finishing and turning and drilling.
We paint a wet flat, and limit and bore,
While the foreman walks 'round like a Varna Road whore,
Varna Road whore,
Varna Road whore,
While the foreman walks 'round like a Varna Road whore.

The Big Banker who's running our nation,
Claims we are the cause of stagnation.
He sits at his desk on his fat pin-stripped arse,
While we do the donkey work, he counts the brass.
He counts the brass,
He counts the brass,
While we do the donkey work, he counts the brass.

Our trade fluctuates with the season,
That's mainly the cause and the reason;
We organise now and go in with both feet,
For tomorrow we may well be walking the streets,
Walking the streets,
Walking the streets,
For tomorrow we may well be walking the streets.

Investors and financial backers,
Are greedily counting the ackers;
Ten guineas an ounce for a working man's sweat,
Then the bastards begrudge us the wages we get.
Wages we get,
Wages we get,
Then the bastards begrudge us the wages we get.

So a word to you wealthy fat Tories
Who dream up those newspaper stories.
If it's true what they say and we're in the stew;
Then we're the red peppers, the dumplings are you.
Dumplings are you,
Dumplings are you,
Then we're the red peppers, the dumplings are you.

Ian Campbell was born in Aberdeen in 1933, and has lived in Birmingham since 1947. He sings professionally in the West Midlands and has appeared on television frequently. He can be contacted at 82 Featherstone Road, Birmingham 14. The song can be heard on *The Circle Game* LP (Transatlantic Records, 1966, TRA163).

Ian Campbell

THE OLD MAN'S SONG

At the turning of the century I was a boy of five,
Me father went to fight the Boers and never came back alive.
Me mother was left to bring us up, no charity she'd seek;
So she washed and scrubbed and scraped along on seven and six a week.

When I was twelve I left the school and went to find a job,
With growing kids me ma was glad of the extra couple of bob.
I'm sure that better schooling would have stood me in good stead,
But you can't afford refinements when you're struggling for your bread.

And when the great war came along I didn't hesitate,
I took the royal shilling and went off to do me bit.
I lived on mud and tears and blood, three years or thereabouts,
Then I copped some gas in Flanders and got invalided out.

Well when the war was over and we'd settled with the Hun,
We got back into civvies and we thought the fighting done,
We'd won the right to live in peace, but we didn't have such luck,
For soon we found we had to fight for the right to go to work.

In '26 the General Strike found me out on the streets,
Though I'd a wife a' kids by then and their needs I had to meet,
For a brave new world was coming, and the brotherhood of man,
But when the strike was over we were back where we began.

I struggled through the 'thirties, out of work now and again,
I saw the blackshirts marching, and the things they did in Spain,
So I reared me children decent, and I taught them wrong from right,
But Hitler was the lad who came along and taught them how to fight.

My daughter was a landgirl, she got married to a Yank,
And they gave me son a gong for stopping one of Rommel's tanks.
He was wounded just before the end, and convalesced in Rome,
He married an Eyetie nurse and never bothered to come home.

My daughter writes me once a month, a cheerful little note,
About their colour telly and the other things they've got,
She's got a son, a likely lad, he's nearly twenty one,
And she tells me now they've called him up to fight in Vietnam.

We're living on the pension now, it doesn't go too far,
Not much to show for a life that seems like one long bloody war,
When you think of all the wasted lives it makes you want to cry,
I'm not sure how to change things, but by Christ we'll have a try.

This can be heard on *Songs of Alex Glasgow Two* LP (Mawson and Wareham Music, 1975, MWM 1009).

Alex Glasgow

TURNING THE CLOCK BACK

My granny tells me that she's seen it all before,
And at ninety four she's seen a thing or two.
She's seen the stockbrokers all crying,
And the speculators sighing,
And the millionaires relying
On a war to pull them through.
Chorus;
    And they're turning the clock back
    I can hear me granny say;
    Yes they're turning the clock back
    And the working man will pay.

My gran remembers the way it used to be
With Baldwin and MacDonald in the chair.
She fetched the soup from down the kitchen,
Heard the speeches, saw men marching,
Read how Churchill sent the troops in,
Which the papers said was fair.
Chorus;
    And they're turning the clock back
    I can hear me granny say;
    Yes they're turning the clock back
    And the working man will pay.

My granny tells me that they're at it once again;
The nobs can't get their profits quite as high.
And Tom and Dick and Harry
Have forgotten that they carry
On their shoulders all the parasites
That suck their bodies dry.
Chorus;
    And they're turning the clock back
    I can hear me granny say.
    They may call it Social Contract
    But the working man will pay.

My granny tells me that it's getting very late,
And we've got our silly heads stuck in the sand.
She says she's got a feeling
We may very soon be reeling
From the evil dealing jackboots
As the blackshirts haunt the land.
Chorus;
    And they're turning the clock back
    I can hear me granny say
    Yes they're turning the clock back
    And the working man will pay.

Originally entitled *The Price of Coal*. But when Alan Plater, Sid Chaplin and Alex Glasgow got together to write a play on the history and struggles of North East pitmen the chorus from this song suggested a fitting title.

A recorded version can be heard on *Songs of Alex Glasgow* LP (Mawson and Wareham Music 1973, MWM 1006) and the words and music are in the Methuen playscript.

Alex Glasgow

CLOSE THE COAL-HOUSE DOOR

Close the coal-house door, lad, there's blood inside.
Blood from broken hands and feet,
Blood that's dried on pit-black meat,
Blood from hearts that know no beat.
Close the coal-house door, lad, there's blood inside.

Close the coal-house door, lad, there's bones inside.
Mangled, splintered piles of bones,
Buried 'neath a mile of stones,
Not a soul to hear the groans.
Close the coal-house door,lad, there's bones inside.

Close the coal-house door, lad, there's bairns inside,
Bairns that had no time to hide,
Bairns that saw the blackness slide,
Bairns beneath the mountain side.
Close the coal-house door, lad, there's bairns inside.

Close the coal-house door, lad, and stay outside.
Geordie's standin' at the dole,
And Mrs Jackson, like a fool,
Complains about the price of coal.
Close the coal-house door, lad, there's blood inside
    There's bones inside, there's bairns inside, so stay outside.

This Woody Guthrie song tells its own tale. It can be heard
on Woody's *Dust Bowl Ballads* (RCA Victor, 1964, RD 7642,
LPV 502).

Woody Guthrie

VIGILANTE MAN

Have you seen that Vigilante Man?
Have you seen that Vigilante Man?
Have you seen that Vigilante Man?
I've been hearing his name all over the land.

Well, what is a Vigilante Man?
Tell me what is a Vigilante Man?
Has he got a gun and a club in his hand?
Is that a Vigilante Man?

Rainy night, down in the engine house;
Sleeping just as still as a mouse;
Man come along and chased us out in the rain,
Was that a Vigilante Man?

Stormy days we'd pass the time away,
Sleeping in some good warm place;
Man come along and we gave him a little race.
Was that a Vigilante Man?

Preacher Casey was just a working man,
And he said, 'Unite all you working men!'
Killed him in a river, some strange man.
Was that a Vigilante Man?

Oh, why does a Vigilante Man,
Why does a Vigilante Man,
Carry that sawed-off shotgun in his hand?
Would he shoot his brother and sister down?

I rambled around from town to town,
I rambled around from town to town;
And they herded us around like a wild herd of cattle,
Was that the Vigilante Men?

Have you seen that Vigilante Man?
Have you seen that Vigilante Man?
I've heard his name all over the land.

This can be heard in a later version on *Songs of Alex Glasgow* LP (Mawson and Wareham Music, 1973, MWM 1006).

Alex Glasgow

STANDING AT THE DOOR

When me father was a lad,
Unemployment was so bad,
He spent best part of his life down at the dole.
Straight from school to the labour queue,
Raggy clothes and holey shoes,
Combin' pit-heaps for a manky bag o' coal.
Chorus;

> And I'm standin' at the door, at the same old bloody door,
> Waiting for the pay-out, as me father did before.

Nowadays we've got a craze,
To follow clever Keynesian ways,
And computers measure economic growth.
We've got experts milling round,
Writing theories on the pound;
Caring little whether we can buy a loaf.
Chorus;

'Course we didn't like the freeze,
But we really tried to please;
'Cause we made the little cross that put them in.
Down the river we've been sold,
For a pot of cheap Swiss gold,
And we're the ones that suffer for their sins.
Chorus;

Baby, baby, this is true,
I'll be standin' in this queue,
Till the Tyne runs clear and plastic roses sing.
So the next time they come by,
Watch the sky for custard pie,
And tell 'em straight, it's Humperdinck for King!
Chorus;

Employment Office

TRU

Oppenheim wrote the poem after seeing a banner – 'We want bread and roses too' – carried by mill girls in the 1912 Lawrence textile strike.

James Oppenheim (1882-1932) was a poet and novelist. He edited a magazine called *The Seven Arts*. His poems frequently appeared in IWW publications. *Bread and Roses*, like many Wobbly songs, first appeared in *Industrial Solidarity*. For further information about the IWW or Wobblies see page 000. A recorded version of the song can be heard on Gene and Francesca Raskin's *We Work and Sing*, issued by the International Ladies Garment Workers' Union, USA. see page 73. A recorded

James Oppenheim

BREAD AND ROSES

As we come marching, marching in the beauty of the day,
A million darkened kitchens, a thousands mill lofts gray,
Are touched with all the radiance that a sudden sun discloses,
For the people hear us singing; 'Bread and roses! Bread and roses!'

As we come marching, marching, we battle too for men,
For they are women's children, and we mother them again.
Our lives shall not be sweated from birth until life closes;
Hearts starve as well as bodies; give us bread, but give us roses!

As we come marching, marching, unnumbered women dead
Go crying through our singing their ancient cry for bread.
Smart art and love and beauty their drudging spirits knew.
Yes, it is bread we fight for — but we fight for roses too!

As we come marching, marching, we bring the greater days.
The rising of the women means the rising of the race.
No more the drudge and idler — ten that toil where one reposes,
But a sharing of life's glories; Bread and roses! Bread and roses!

Written in 1957. A year earlier Timothy Evans was hanged for the murder of his wife. In 1957 the mass murderer Christie (Evans's landlord) confessed to the crime.
    A recorded version of this song can be found on *Chorus from the Gallows* (Topic Records, 1960, 12T16).

Ewan MacColl

GO DOWN YOU MURDERERS

Tim Evans was a prisoner fast in his prison cell,
And those who read about his crimes, they damned his soul to hell.
Saying, 'Go down you murderer, go down!'

For the murder of his own dear wife and the killing of his own child.
The jury found him guilty and the hanging judge he smiled,
Saying, 'Go down you murderer, go down!'

Evans pleaded innocent and he swore by Him on high,
That he never killed his own dear wife nor caused his child to die
Saying, 'Go down you murderer, go down!'

So they moved him out of C block to his final *flowery dell*,
And the day and night two *screws* were there, and they never left his cell,
Saying, 'Go down you murderer, go down!'

Sometimes they played draughts with him and solo and pontoon,
To stop him brooding on the rope that was to be his doom,
Saying, 'Go down you murderer, go down!'

They brought his grub in on a tray, there were eggs and meat and ham,
And all the *snout* that he could smoke was there at his command,
Saying, 'Go down you murderer, go down!'

Evans walked in the prison yard and the screws they walked behind,
And he saw the sky above the wall but he knew no peace of mind,
Saying, 'Go down you murderer, go down!'

They came for him at eight o'clock and the chaplain read a prayer,
And then they walked him to that place where the hangman did prepare,
Saying, 'Go down you murderer, go down!'

The rope was fixed around his neck and a washer behind his ear,
And the prison bell was tolling, but Tim Evans did not hear,
Saying, 'Go down you murderer, go down!'

A thousand *lags* were cursing and a-banging on the doors,
Tim Evans did not hear them, he was deaf forevermore,
Saying, 'Go down you murderer, go down!'

They sent Tim Evans to the *drop* for a crime he didn't do,
It was Christie was the murderer and the judge and jury too,
Saying, 'Go down you murderers, go down.'

This song can be heard on *The World Of Ewan MacColl and Peggy Seeger* (Argo SPA-A 102) as well as on the hit single, recorded almost twenty years after the song was written, by *Roberta Flack* (Atlantic Records, K10161).

Ewan MacColl

THE FIRST TIME EVER I SAW YOUR FACE

The first time ever I saw your face,
I thought the sun rose in your eyes,
And the moon and stars were the gifts you gave,
To the dark and empty skies, my love,
To the dark and empty skies.

The first time ever I kissed your mouth,
I felt the earth move in my hand,
Like a trembling heart of a captive bird
That was there at my command, my love,
That was there at my command.

The first time ever I lay with you,
And felt your heart beat close to mine,
I thought our joy would fill the earth
And last till the end of time, my love,
And last till the end of time.

Chemical process workers remained unsung until Ron Angel, songwriter of the Teesside Fettlers, wrote this anthem. The Fettlers can be contacted via Ron Angel. Middlesbrough (0642) 87261.

Ron Angel

CHEMICAL WORKERS

A process man am I and I'm tell you no lie.
I work and breathe amongst the fumes that trail across the sky.
There's thunder all around me and poison in the air;
There's a lousy smell that smacks of Hell and dust all in me hair.
Chorus;

> And it's go boys, go;
> They'll time your every breath.
> And every day you're in this place
> You're two days nearer death,
> But you go.

I've worked amongst the spinners, I've breathed in the oily smoke.
I've shovelled up the gypsum that nigh on makes you choke.
I've stood knee deep in cyanide, gone sick with a caustic burn;
Been working rough and seen enough to make your stomach turn.
Chorus;

There's overtime and bonus, opportunities galore.
Young lads like the money, and they all come back for more.
But soon you're knocking on and look older than you should;
For every bob made on this job you pay with flesh and blood.
Chorus;

Written when Hugh Gaitskell led the Labour Party. It is still relevant. Sung to a distorted version of Maryland it is a parody of *The Red Flag*.

Leon Rosselson began his singing-songwriting career with the Galliards. When they broke up he struck out on his own, writing and singing political satires before the 'satire boom' of the sixties, and then as part of it. He kept on after it had subsided. He sings in clubs, pubs, colleges and universities, as well as on radio and television.

Leon's songs can be found in *Look Here*, and *That's Not the Way It's Got To Be* (both distributed by (the Publications Distribution Cooperative) and can be heard on *The Word is Hugga Mugga Chugga Lugga Humbugga Boom Chit* (Trailer LER 3015) and *Palaces of Gold* (Acorn CF 249), and with Roy Bailey, on *That's Not the Way It's Got To Be* (Acorn CF 251) and on *Love, Loneliness and Laundry* (Acorn CF 271). Leon can be contacted at 01- 902 0655.

Leon Rosselson

BATTLE HYMN OF THE NEW SOCIALIST PARTY

The cloth cap and the working class
As images are dated
For we are Labour's avant-garde
And we were educated.
By tax adjustments we have planned
To institute the promised land.
And just to show we're still sincere
We sing *The Red Flag* once a year.

44

Firm principles and policies
Are open to objections.
And a streamlined party image is
The way to win elections.
So raise the umbrella high
The bowler hat and college tie.
We'll stand united, raise a cheer
And sing *The Red Flag* once a year.

It's one step forward, one step back
Our dance is devilish daring.
A leftward shuffle, a rightward tack,
The pause to take our bearings.
We'll reform the country, bit by bit
So nobody will notice it.
Then ever after, never fear
We'll sing *The Red Flag* once a year.

We will not cease from mental fight
Till every wrong is righted.
And all men are equal quite,
And all our leaders knighted.
For we are sure if we persist
To make the New Year's Honours List.
Then every loyal Labour Peer
Will sing *The Red Flag* once a year.

So vote for us, and not for them
We're just as true to N.A.T.O.
We'll be as calm and British when
We steer the ship of state — O.
We'll stand as firm as them
To show we're patriotic gentlemen
Though man to man shall brothers be;
Deterrence is our policy.

So raise the mushroom clouds on high
Within their shade we'll live — and die
Though cowards flinch and traitors sneer,
We'll sing *The Red Flag* once a year.

Peggy is the sister of the US songwriter and singer, Pete Seeger, and daughter of Charles Seeger, an eminent musicologist. She was born in New York City in 1935, and went to Radcliffe College. In 1955, she left the US to visit Europe and Asia; and in 1956 she met Ewan MacColl, whom she later married.

This song is in *New City Songster* Volume 7 and can be heard, sung by Peggy Seeger, on *At The Present Moment* LP (Rounder Records, USA, 1973, 4003). Both are available from 35 Stanley Avenue, Beckenham, Kent.

Peggy Seeger

I'M GONNA BE AN ENGINEER

When I was a little girl I wished I was a boy,
I lagged along behind the gang and wore my corduroys.
Everybody said I only did it to annoy,
But I was gonna be an engineer.
Momma told me 'Can't you be a Lady?
Your duty is to make me the mother of a pearl.
Wait until you're older, dear and maybe
You'll be glad that you're a girl.'
   Dainty as a Dresden statue,
   Gentle as a Jersey cow,
   Smooth as silk,
   Gives creamy milk.
   Learn to coo,
   Learn to moo;
   That's what to do to be a lady now.

When I went to school I learned to write and how to read
Some history and geography and home economy;
And typing is a skill that every girl is sure to need,
To while away the extra time until the time to breed.
And then they had the nerve to say; 'What would you like to be?'
I says, 'I'm gonna be an engineer!'
'No, you only need to learn to be a lady
The duty isn't yours, for to try and run the world.
An engineer could never have a baby,
Remember, dear, that you're a girl.'

So I become a typist and I study on the sly,
Working out the day and night so I can qualify.
And every time the boss come in, he pinched me on the thigh,
Says; 'I've never had an engineer!'
You owe it to the job to be a lady
It's the duty of the staff for to give the boss a whirl
The wages that you get are crummy, maybe
But it's all you get, 'cause you're a girl.
   She's smart! (for a woman)
   I wonder how she got that way?
   You get no choice
   You get no voice
   Just stay mum
   Pretend you're dumb
   That's how you come to be a lady today!

Then Jimmy come along and we set up a conjugation,
We were busy every night with loving recreation.
I spent my days at work so he could get his education,
And now he's an engineer!

He says; 'I know you'll always be a lady.
It's the duty of my darling to love me all her life.
Could an engineer look after or obey me?
Remember, dear, that you're my wife!

As soon as Jimmy got a job I studied hard again,
Then, busy at me turret lathe a year or so, and then,
The morning that the twins were born, Jimmy says to them,
'Kids, your mother was an engineer!'
You owe it to the kids to be a lady;
Dainty as a dishrag, faithful as a chow,
Stay at home you got to mind the baby,
Remember you're a mother now.

Every time I turn around there's something else to do,
Cook a meal or mend a sock or sweep a floor or two.
Listen in to Jimmy Young — it makes me want to spew
I was gonna be an engineer!
I really wish that I could be a lady,
I could do the lovely things that a lady's s'posed to do.
I wouldn't even mind if only they would pay me,
And I could be a person too.
    What price — for a woman?
    You can buy her for a ring of gold;
    To love and obey,
    (Without any pay)
    You get a cook or a nurse
    For better or worse
    You don't need a purse when a lady is sold!

But now that times are harder, and my Jimmy's got the sack,
I went down to Vickers, they were glad to have me back,
I'm a third class citizen, my wages tell me that.
But I'm a first class engineer!
The boss he says; 'I pay you as a lady,
You only got the job 'cause I can't afford a man.
With you I keep the profits high as may be;
You're just a cheaper pair of hands!'
    You got one fault! You're a woman.
    You're not worth the equal pay.
    A bitch or a tart,
    You're nothing but heart
    Shallow and vain,
    You got no brain;
    Go down the drain like a lady today!

I listened to my mother and I joined a typing pool,
I listened to my lover and I sent him through his school.
If I listen to the boss, I'm just a bloody fool;
And an underpaid engineer!
I've been a sucker ever since I was a baby.
As a daughter, as a wife, as a mother, and a dear —
But I'll fight them as a woman, not a lady,
I'll fight them as an engineer!

A spirited version can be heard on *Bundock Ballads* (Topic Records, 12T130).

JOIN THE BRITISH ARMY

When I was young I used to be
As fine a man as ever you'd see.
The Prince of Wales he said to me,
Come and join the British Army.
   Too-ral-loo-ral-loo-ral-loo
   They're looking for monkeys up in the zoo
   And if I had a face like you
   I'd join the British Army.

Sarah Condon baked a cake.
'Twas all for poor old Slattery's sake.
I threw myself into the lake;
Pretending I was barmy.
   Too-ral-loo-ral-loo-ral-loo
   'Twas the only thing that I could do
   To work my ticket[1] home to you
   And leave the British Army.

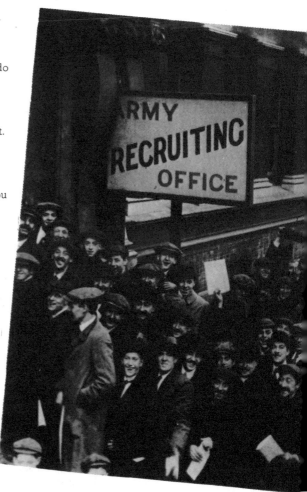

Corporal Daly's got such a drought,
Just give him a couple of jars of stout.
He'll kill the enemy with his mouth,
And save the British Army.
   Too-ral-loo-ral-loo-ral-loo
   My curses on the labour-broo[2]
   That took my darling boy from you
   To join the British Army.

Captain Johnson went away
And his wife got in the family way.
And all the words that she could say
Was blame the British Army.
   Too-ral-loo-ral-loo-ral-loo,
   I've made my mind up what to do,
   I'll work my ticket home to you,
   And leave the British Army.

1. obtain discharge notice
2. Labour Exchange

McAlpine is one of Britain's biggest and most ruthless construction empires.

Dominic Behan is one of the best known living Irish songsters. His uncle wrote the Irish national anthem and his brother was the playwright Brendan Behan. McAlpine's Fusiliers is on *The Very Best of the Dubliners* (EMC 3146). Dominic can be contacted at Harpenden Cottage, Dublin, Lanarkshire.

Dominic Behan

McALPINE'S FUSILIERS

As down the glen rode McAlpine's men
With their shovels slung behind them.
'Twas in the pub that they drank their sub,
And up in the spike you'll find them.
They sweated blood and they washed down mud
With pints and quarts of beer,
And now we are on the road again
With McAlpine's Fusiliers.

I've stripped to the skin with Darkie Finn
Down upon the Isle of Grain.
With Horseface Toole I knew the rule;
No bonus if you stopped for rain.
While McAlpine's god was a well-filled hod
With your shoulders cut and seared,
And woe to he went to look for tea
With McAlpine's Fusiliers.

I mind the day when the bear O'Shea
Fell into a concrete stair.
What Horseface said when he saw him dead
Wasn't what the rich call prayers.
I'm a navvy short was the one retort
That reached unto my ears.
When the going is rough you must be tough
With McAlpine's Fusiliers.

I've worked 'till sweat has had me bet
With Russian, Czech and Pole;
On the shuttering jams upon the hydro dams,
Or down below the Thames in a hole.
I've grafted hard and I've got my cards
And many a ganger's fist across my ears.
If you pride your life don't join, by Christ,
With McAlpine's Fusiliers.

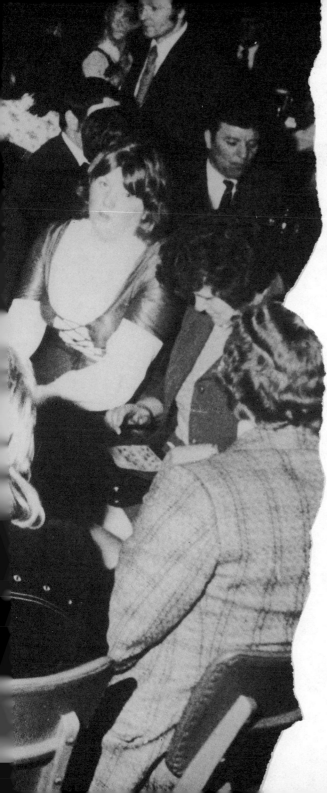

Alex Glasgow was born the son of a
pitman in Gateshead in 1935. He went
to Leeds University, then as a language
assistant to Germany, where he did some
schools' radio and recorded a hit single.
Back on Tyneside in the late 'fifties he
worked freelance for radio and began to
write songs. He has recently turned his
hand to writing plays in the highly
successful TV series *When The Boat
Comes In.*

A recorded version of this song can
be heard on *Songs of Alex Glasgow,*
Mawson and Wareham Music, Blackett
St, Newcastle (1973, MWM 1006). Alex
can be contacted at 59 Church Rd, Low
Fell, Gateshead (0632 878337).

Alex Glasgow

AS SOON AS THIS PUB CLOSES

I could have done it yesterday,
If I hadn't had a cold
But since I've put this pint away
I've never felt so bold
So — as soon as this pub closes
As soon as this pub closes
As soon as this pub closes
The Revolution starts.

I'll shoot the aristocracy
And confiscate their brass
Create a fine democracy
That's truly working class.
As soon as this pub closes
As soon as this pub closes
As soon as this pub closes
I'll raise the banner high.

I'll fight the nasty racialists
And scrap the colour bar
And all fascist dictatorships
And every commissar
As soon as this pub closes
As soon as this pub closes
As soon as this pub closes
I'll man the barricades.

So raise your glasses everyone
For everything is planned
And each and every mother's son
Will see the promised land
As soon as this pub closes
As soon as this pub closes
As soon as this pub closes
. . .I think I'm gonna be sick.

Written (or so the story goes) in 1844 as a warning to
potential scabs who were being imported into the
North East coalfields from as far away as Cornwall and
Ireland.

   Many variations of this song exist. The most
familiar is probably that found in *Come All Ye Bold
Miners* edited by A.L. Lloyd (1952), which differs
from that given in his *Folksong in England* (Lawrence
and Wishart, 1967). Louis Killen can be heard singing
The Blackleg Miner on *The Iron Muse* (Topic Records,
1956, 12T86).

THE BLACKLEG MINER

It's in the evenin' after dark
When a blackleg miner creeps te work
With his moleskin pants and dorty shirt
There goes the blackleg miner.

He'll take his picks and down he goes
Te hew the coal that lies below
But there's not a woman in this town row
Will look at a blackleg miner.

Now, divvent gan[1] near the Delavel mine
Across the way they stretch a line
Te catch the throat an' break the spine
Of the dorty blackleg miner.

An' Seghill is a terrible place
They rub wet clay in a blackleg's face
An' around the heap they run a foot race
Te catch the blackleg miner.

They take ye duds an' tools as well
An' hoy[2] them doon the pit of hell
Down ye go an' fare ye well
Ye dorty blackleg miner.

So join the union while ye may
Don't wait till yer dyin' day
'Cause that may not be far away
Ye dorty blackleg miner.

1. don't go
2. throw

52

The first Penal Code was introduced by the
British in Ireland in 1692 and embellished over the
next two centuries. Its aims were simple; to deny
Catholics any legal rights, to suppress their
political and religious organisations and to grant
the authorities unlimited powers of search and
arrest in order to keep the 'croppies' in their place.
As so often happens in colonial situations the
agents of foreign repression — in this case the
Royal Irish Constabulary — were characterised by
their arrogant abuses of power and their stupidity.
   A fine version of this song can be heard sung
by Dominic Behan on *Peelers & Prisoners* EP
(Topic Records, 1963, TOP 85).

THE PEELERS AND THE GOAT

Oh the Bansha peelers went one night
On duty at the trowning — O
They met a goat upon the road,
And took him for being a strolling — O
With bayonets fixed, they sallied forth
And commandeered the whizzen — O
And they they swore out a mighty oath;
They sent him off to prison — O

'Oh mercy sir,' the goat replied,
'And let me tell me story — O
Sure I'm no rogue or ribon man,[1]
Nor croppie,[2] Whig or Tory — O
I'm guilty not of any crime;
Of petty or high treason — O
And our tribe is wanted at this time;
For this is the ranting season — O'.

'It is in vain for to complain,
Or give your tongue such bridle — O
You're absent from your dwelling place,
Disorderly and idle — O
Your hoary locks will not prevail,
Nor your sublime oration — O
For Penal Laws will you transport
On your own information — O'

'No Penal Laws did I transgress,
By deed or combination[3] — O
I have no certain place of rest;
Nor home or habitation — O
But Bansha is my dwelling place,
Where I was born and bred — O
I descended from an honest race;
That's all the trade I've leaden — O'

'I will chastise your insolence
And violent behaviour — O
Well bound to Cashell[4] you'll be sent
Where you will gain no favour — O
The magistrates will all consent
To sign your condemnation — O
From there to Cork you will be sent
For speedy transportation — O'

'This parish and this neighbourhood
Are peaceable and tranquil — O
There's no disturbance here, thank God,
And long may it continue — so.
I don't regard your author pin,
And sign for my committal — O
My jury will be gentlemen
And grant me my acquittal — O'

'The consequence be what it will,
The peeler's power, I'll let you know,
I'll handcuff you at all events
And march you to the Bridewell[4] — O
And sure, you rogue, you can't deny
Before the judge or jury — O
Intimidation with your horns,
And threatening me with fury — O'

'I make no doubt that you are drunk,
With whiskey, rum or brandy — O
Or you wouldn't have such gallant spunk
To be so bald or manly — O
You readily would let me pass
If I had money handy — O
To treat you to a potcheen glass,
Oh 'tis then I'd be the dandy — O.'

1. member of secret peasant society in 18th century Ireland
2. Catholic peasant farmer
3. conspiracy
4. a prison

Joe Hill was the most prolific of Wobbly songsters and their most famous martyr. Born Joel Hillström he migrated to America in 1901 from Sweden and joined the IWW in 1911 (see page 72). He spent the next three years as a migrant worker and IWW organiser. In 1914, Joe Hill was framed on a murder charge and sentenced to death. Despite a worldwide campaign to free him he was shot by firing squad on 19th November 1915.

On the eve of execution he wrote to Big Bill Haywood, the General Secretary of the IWW saying 'Don't waste time mourning. Organise.' Haywood replied 'Goodbye Joe. You will live in the hearts of the working class. Your songs will be sung wherever workers toil.'

The Preacher and the Slave was printed in the third edition of the *IWW Songbook* and sung to the hymn tune 'Sweet Bye and Bye.' 'Here, if anywhere, was a clear breach with timidity, moralism and the whole manner and content of the standard American Culture.' Henry F May, *The End of American Innocence.*

Joe Hill

THE PREACHER AND THE SLAVE

Long haired preachers come out every night,
Try to tell you what's wrong and what's right;
But when asked how 'bout something to eat,
They will answer with voices so sweet;
Chorus;
   You will eat, bye and bye,
   In that glorious land above the sky.
   Work and pray, live on hay,
   You'll get pie in the sky when you die.

And the starvation army they play,
And they sing and they clap and they pray.
Till they get all your coin on the drum,
Then they tell you when you're on the bum;
Chorus;

If you fight hard for children and wife —
Try to get something good in this life.
You're a sinner and bad man, they tell,
When you die you will sure go to hell.
Chorus;

Workingmen of all countries unite,
Side by side we for freedom will fight;
When the world and its wealth we have gained,
To the grafters we'll sing this refrain;
Final Chorus;
   You will eat, bye and bye;
   When you've learned how to cook and to fry.
   Chop some wood, 'twill do you good,
   And you'll eat in the sweet bye and bye.

A Wobbly song. Sung first by US troops during the Spanish American War, the song was taken up by loggers in the North West and 'harvest stiffs'. Its authorship was unknown until 1926 when the veteran Wobbly Harry McClintock claimed it. (For the Wobblies, see page 72).

First published in the April 1908 issue of the *Industrial Union Bulletin.* A recorded version of the song can be found on *Songs of the Wobblies* LP by Joe Glazier and Bill Friedland, Labor Arts 3.

Harry McClintock

HALLELUJAH I'M A BUM

Oh, why don't you work
Like other men do?
How in hell can I work
When there's no work to do?
Chorus;
   Hallelujah, I'm a bum!
   Hallelujah, bum again!
   Hallelujah, give us a handout
   To revive us again.

Oh, why don't you save
All the money you earn?
If I did not eat
I'd have money to burn.
Chorus;

Oh, I like my boss —
He's a good friend of mine;
That's why I am starving
Out in the breadline.
Chorus;

I can't buy a job
For I ain't got the dough,
So I ride in a box-car
For I'm a hobo.
Chorus;

Whenever I get
All the money I earn
The boss will be broke
And to work he must turn.
Chorus;

This was sung in 1933 by the inmates of Nazi concentration camps. It originated either from Börgermoor or Dachau when those camps were being used chiefly for political prisoners.

The song can be heard on *Songs of Protest* EP by the Ian Campbell Folk Group EP (Topic Records, 1962, TOP 82).

THE PEAT-BOG SOLDIERS

Far and wide as the eye can wander,
Heath and bog are everywhere.
Not a bird sings out to cheer us,
Oaks are standing gaunt and bare.
Chorus;
    We are the peat-bog soldiers;
    We're marching with our spades
    To the moor.

Up and down the guards are pacing;
No one, no one can go through.
Flight would mean a sure death facing,
Guns and barbed wire greet our view.
Chorus;

But for us there's no complaining,
Winter will in time be past.
One day we shall cry rejoicing,
Homeland, dear you're mine at last.
Final chorus;
    Then will the peat-bog soldiers
    March no more with their spades
    To the moor.

First published by the Workers' Music Association in 1939. By 1955 it had entered the *Labour Party Songbook*. It can be heard on Joe Glazer's *Songs of Work & Freedom* (Washington Records, USA, WR 460).

Paddy Ryan

THE MAN THAT WATERS THE WORKERS' BEER

Chorus;
I'm the man, the very fat man, that waters the workers' beer.
Yes, I'm the man, the very fat man, that waters the workers' beer.
What do I care if it makes them ill, or it makes them terribly queer?
I've a car, a yacht, and an aeroplane and I waters the workers' beer.

Now, when I makes the workers' beer I puts in strychinine;
Some methylated sprits and a drop of paraffine.
But since a brew so terribly strong might make them terribly queer;
I reaches my hand for the water tap and I waters the workers' beer!
Chorus;

Now, a drop of good beer is good for a man who's thirsty and tired and hot,
And I sometimes has a drop for myself from a very special lot.
But a fat and healthy working class is the thing that I most fear;
So I reaches my hand for my water tap and I waters the workers' beer.
Chorus;

Now, ladies, fair, beyond compare, and be ye maid or wife.
Oh, sometimes lend a thought for me who leads a wand'ring life.
The water rates are shockingly high, and the 'meth' is shockingly dear.
And there isn't the profit there used to be in wat'ring the workers' beer!

The origins of this song are obscure, although the reference to 'Don John' probably dates it to the time of the War of Spanish Succession (1701-12).

MRS McGRATH

'Oh Mrs McGrath!' the sergeant said,
'Would you like to make a soldier
   out of your son Ted?
With a scarlet coat and a big cocked hat?
Now, Mrs McGrath, wouldn't you like that?'
Chorus;
   With your too-ri-aa,
   fol-the-diddle-aa,
   Too-ri-oo-ri-oo-ri-aa,
   (Repeat)

So Mrs McGrath lived on the sea-shore,
For the space of seven long years or more,
Till she saw a big ship sailing into the bay,
'Here's my son, Ted, wisha, clear the way.'
Chorus;

'Oh, Captain dear, where have you been?
Have you been sailing on the Mediterreen?
Or have ye any tidings of my son Ted,
Is the poor boy living, or is he dead?'
Chorus;

Then up comes Ted without any legs,
And in their place he has two wooden pegs,
She kissed him a dozen times or two,
Saying, 'Holy Moses, 'tisn't you.'
Chorus;

'Oh then were ye drunk, or were ye blind,
That ye left ye two fine legs behind?
Or was it walking upon the sea
Wore ye two fine legs from the knees away?'
Chorus;

'Oh I wasn't drunk, and I wasn't blind
But I left my two fine legs behind.
For a cannon ball on the fifth of May
Took my two fine legs from the knees away.'
Chorus;

'Oh then, Teddy me boy!' the widow cried,
'Ye two fine legs were ye mammy's pride.
Them stumps of a tree wouldn't do at all,
Why didn't ye run from the big cannon ball?'
Chorus;

'All foreign wars I do proclaim
Between Don John and the King of Spain.
And by herrins I'll make them rue the time
That they swept the legs from a child of mine.'
Chorus;

'Oh then, if I had you back again,
I'd never let you go to fight the King of Spain.
For I'd rather my Ted as he used to be
Than the King of France and his whole Navee.'
Chorus;

Written by Woody Guthrie after he and Pete Seeger had visited a union meeting in Oklahoma in 1940. The meeting was attacked by company thugs who were eventually driven off by a woman member and members of the Ladies' Auxiliary — an organisation of union wives.

Woody Guthrie was born in Oklahoma in 1912. He spent much of his early life wandering the Western States as a hobo musician, playing to cowboys in Texas and union meetings in California. In the late 'thirties he moved to New York and worked for the *Daily Worker*. He is estimated to have written over a thousand songs which have now been published by Oak Publishers, New York. Guthrie's songs were composed largely for workers, dirt farmers and racial minorities. In the 'forties he joined forces with Seeger and Cico Houston to form the Almanac Singers which greatly influenced the post war folk song revival. It is hardly surprising then that the 'protest' singers of the early 'sixties turned to Guthrie for advice and inspiration. Woody Guthrie died of Huntingdon's Chorea in 1967. His life story can be read in *Bound For Glory* (Paladin).

Nancy Katz's alternative third verse is included for obvious reasons, but it is included and not substituted; for we believe that today's socialists will get nowhere by ignoring the uncomfortable truth that even 'heroes' like Woody Guthrie were flawed by incipient male chauvinism.

A recorded version by the Almanac Singers is to be heard on *The Original Talking Union* LP (Folkways Records, FH 5285).

Woody Guthrie

UNION MAID

There once was a union maid who never was afraid
Of goons and ginks and company finks and the deputy sheriffs that made the raid
She went to the union hall, when a meeting it was called,
And when the company boys came around she always stood her ground.
Chorus;
    Oh, you can't scare me, I'm sticking to the union;
    I'm sticking to the union, I'm sticking to the union.
    Oh, you can't scare me, I'm sticking to the union,
    I'm sticking to the union 'til the day I die.

This union maid was wise to the tricks of the company spies;
She never got fooled by a company stool, she'd always organise the guys.
She'd always get her way when she struck for higher pay;
She'd show her card to the company guard and this is what she'd say;
Chorus;

You gals who want to be free just take a little tip from me:
Get you a man who's a union man and join the Ladies' Auxiliary;
Married life ain't hard when you've got a union card,
A union man has a happy life when he's got a union wife.

** A woman's struggle is hard, even with a union card;
She's got to stand on her own two feet and not
be a servant of a male élite.
It's time to take a stand, keep working hand in hand,
There is a job that's got to be done, and a fight
that's got to be won.
Chorus;

**The alternative third verse was written by Nancy Katz and published in the 1973 edition of the IWW Songbook.

This song can be found on *Matt McGinn Again* (Transatlantic Records, XTRA 1057).

Matt McGinn

THREE NIGHTS AND A SUNDAY DOUBLE-TIME

There's a fellow down the road that I avoid;
He's one of them they call the unemployed.
He says it's all because of me,
He can't get a job when I've got three;
I've three nights and a Sunday double time.
Chorus;
    Three nights and a Sunday double time.
    I work all day, and I work all night;
    To hell wi' you, Jack, I'm all right,
    I've three nights and a Sunday double time.

The wife came to the works the other day,
Said she, 'We've another wee one on the way.'
Says I, 'Nae wonder you can laugh —
I've no been hame for a year and a half!'
I've three nights and a Sunday double time.
Chorus;

They've gone and introduced a new machine,
There's ten men where they once had seventeen.
The machine does the work of four you see,
And I do the work of the other three,
I've three nights and a Sunday double time.
Chorus;

I've a big Post Office book it's true,
I must be worth a fiver more than you.
I saved by eating potted head —
It'll pay for the hearse when I drop dead.
I've three nights and a Sunday double time.
Chorus;

I never miss the pub on a Friday night,
And there you'll always find me gay and bright.
You'll see me down at the old Pack Horse —
I'm a weekend waiter there of course.
I've three nights and a Sunday double time.
Chorus;

Some'll head for heaven when they die,
To find a Dunlopillo in the sky.
But I'll be going to the other place,
For an idle life I couldn't face.
I've three nights and a Sunday double time.
Chorus;

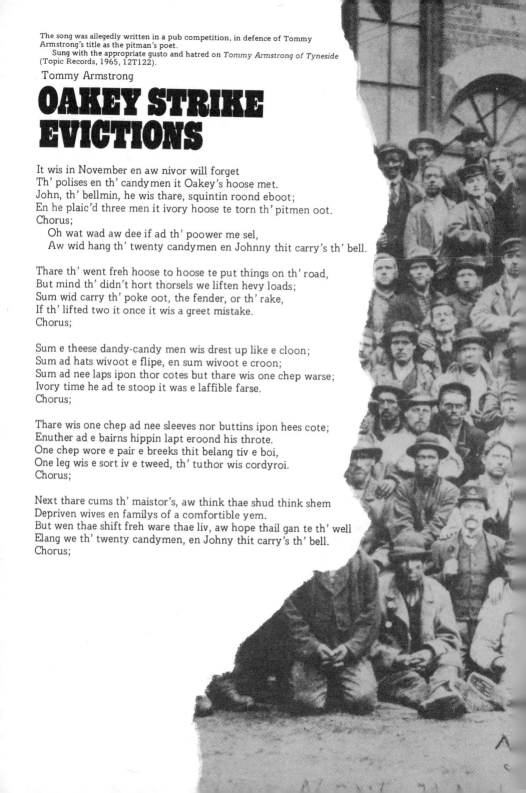

The song was allegedly written in a pub competition, in defence of Tommy
Armstrong's title as the pitman's poet.
Sung with the appropriate gusto and hatred on *Tommy Armstrong of Tyneside*
(Topic Records, 1965, 12T122).

Tommy Armstrong

OAKEY STRIKE EVICTIONS

It wis in November en aw nivor will forget
Th' polises en th' candymen it Oakey's hoose met.
John, th' bellmin, he wis thare, squintin roond eboot;
En he plaic'd three men it ivory hoose te torn th' pitmen oot.
Chorus;
    Oh wat wad aw dee if ad th' poower me sel,
    Aw wid hang th' twenty candymen en Johnny thit carry's th' bell.

Thare th' went freh hoose to hoose te put things on th' road,
But mind th' didn't hort thorsels we liften hevy loads;
Sum wid carry th' poke oot, the fender, or th' rake,
If th' lifted two it once it wis a greet mistake.
Chorus;

Sum e theese dandy-candy men wis drest up like e cloon;
Sum ad hats wivoot e flipe, en sum wivoot e croon;
Sum ad nee laps ipon thor cotes but thare wis one chep warse;
Ivory time he ad te stoop it was e laffible farse.
Chorus;

Thare wis one chep ad nee sleeves nor buttins ipon hees cote;
Enuther ad e bairns hippin lapt eroond his throte.
One chep wore e pair e breeks thit belang tiv e boi,
One leg wis e sort iv e tweed, th' tuthor wis cordyroi.
Chorus;

Next thare cums th' maistor's, aw think thae shud think shem
Depriven wives en familys of a comfortible yem.
But wen thae shift freh ware thae liv, aw hope thail gan te th' well
Elang we th' twenty candymen, en Johny thit carry's th' bell.
Chorus;

Sometimes known by its later title of *Jone o'Grinfilt Jnr — The Four Loom Weaver* came out of the struggles and hardships of Lancashire cotton weavers in the years after 1815, when the bosses tried to offset a decline in trade by cutting wages and using women and kids to force out the highly skilled weavers.

There exist many versions of this song; *The Four Loom Weaver* on *Steam Whistle Ballads* (Topic Records, 1958, 12T104) converts the original irony and underlying hate into dramatised sentiment. Our version is taken from *Ballads & Songs of Lancashire* (1882), edited by John Harland and T.T. Wilkinson, where the rest of the Jone o'Grinfilt songs can be read. The best recorded version is available on *The Iron Muse* (Topic Records, 12T86).

THE FOUR LOOM WEAVER

Aw'm a poor cotton-wayver, as money a one knaws,
Aw've nowt t'ate i' th' heawse, un 'aw've worn eawt my cloas,
You'd hardly gie sixpence fur o' aw've got on,
Meh clogs ur' booath baws'n, un' stockings aw've none;
You'd think it wur hard, to be sent into th' ward
To clem[1] un' do best 'ot yo' con.

Eawr parish-church pa'son's kept telling us lung.
We'st see better toimes, if aw'd but howd my tung;
Aw've howden my tung, till aw con hardly draw breoth
Aw think i my heart he meons t' clem me to deoth;
Aw knaw he lives weel, wi' backbitin' the de'il
Bur he never pick'd o'er in his loife.

Wey tooart on six week, thinkin' aich day wur th' last,
Wey tarried un' shifted, till neaw wey're quite fast;
Wey liv't upon nettles, whoile nettles were good;
Un' Wayterloo porritch[2] wur' th' best o' us food;
Aw'm tellin yo' true, aw con foind foak enoo
Thot're livin' no better nur me.

Neaw, owd Bill o'Dan's sent bailies[3] one day,
Fur t' shop scoar aw'd ow'd him, 'ot aw' couldn't pay;
Bur he're just to lat, fur owd Bill o' Bent,
Had sent eit'un cart, un' ta'en goods fur t'rent.
They laft nowt bur a stool ot're seeots for two,
Un' on it sat Marget un' me.

The bailies sceawlt reawnd us os sly os a meawse,
When they seedn 'o th' things wur ta'en eawt o' the heawse;
Un' t' one says to th' tother, 'O's gone, theaw may see.'
Aw said 'Never fret lads, you're welcome ta' me;'
They made no moor ado, bur ipt up th'owd stoo',
Un' wey booath leeten swack upon th' flags[4].

Aw geet howd o' eawr Marget, for hoo're strucken sick,
Hoo said, hoo'd ne'er had sich a ba-g sin' hoo're wick,
The bailies sceawrt off, wi' th' owd stoo' on their back,
Un they wouldn't ha'e caret if they'd brokken her neck.
They'rn so made at own Bent, 'cos he'd ta'en goods fur rent,
Till they'rn ready to flee us alive.

1. starve
2. Waterloo porridge, an anaemic stew of grass etc.
3. bailiffs
4. fell on the floor
5. work
6. London

64

Aw said to eawr Marget, as wey lien upon th' floor,
'Wey ne'er shall be lower i' this wo'ald, aw'm sure,
Fur if wey mun alter, aw'm sure wey mum mend,
Fur aw think i' my heart wey're booath at fur end,
Fur mayt wey han none, nur no looms to wayve on,
Ecod! th' looms are as well lost as fun.'

My piece wur cheeont off, un' aw took it him back;
Aw hardly durst spake, mester looked so black —
He said; 'Yo're o'erpaid last 'oime 'ot you coom.'
Aw said, 'If aw'wur, 'twui wi' wayving beawt loom;
Un i' t' moind 'ot aw'm in, aw'st ne'er pick o'er again,
For aw've wooven mysel' to th' fur end.'

So aw coom eawt o' th' wareheawse, un' laft him chew that,
When aw thowt 'ot o' things, aw're so vext that aw swat;
Fur to think aw mun warch , to keep him un' o' th' set,
O' th' days o' my loife, un' then dee i' th'r debt;
But aw'll give o'er this made, un' work wi' a spade,
Or goo un' break stone upo' th' road.

Eawr Marget declares, if hoo'd cloas to put on,
Hoo'd go up to Lunnen   to see the great mon;
Un' if things did no' awter, when theere hoo had been,
Hoo says hoo'd begin, un' feight blood up to th' e'en,
Hoo's nout agen th' King, bur hoo loikes a fair thing,
Un' hoo says hoo con tell when hoo's hurt.

Ed Pickford is a schoolteacher living near Sunderland, and a former member with
Nick Fenwick and Mike Elliot of the Northern Front 'folksinging' group. His
songs have been used for many years in clubs in the North East and elsewhere, yet
only recently has he been able to produce his first solo LP — *Songwriter* (Ripoff
Records, 1976, ROF 001). Ed can be contacted at 4 Cedars Park, Ryhope Road,
Sunderland, Tyne and Wear.

Ed Pickford

THE POUND-A-WEEK RISE

Come all you colliers who work down the mine,
From Scotland to Southwich, from Teesdale to Tyne.
I'll sing you the song of the pound-a-week rise
And the men who were fooled by the government lies.
Chorus;
    So it's down you go, down below, Jack,
    Where you never see the skies,
    And you're working in a dungeon
    For your pound-a-week rise.

In nineteen and sixty, not three years ago,
The mine-workers' leaders to Lord Robens did go,
Saying, 'We work very hard, every day we risk our lives,
And we ask you, here and now, for a pound-a-week rise.'
Chorus;

Then up spoke Lord Robens and made this decree;
'When the output rises, then with you I will agree
To raise up your wages and give to you fair pay,
For I was once a miner and worked hard in my day.'
Chorus;

The miners they went home and they worked hard and well;
And their lungs filled with coal-dust in the bosom of Hell,
And the output rose by fifteen, eighteen per cent and more,
And when two years had passed and gone, it rose above a score.
Chorus;

So the mine-workers' leaders went to get their hard-won prize,
And to ask Lord Robens for the pound-a-week rise.
But Robens wouldn't give a pound, he wouldn't give ten bob,
He gave them seven and six and said, 'Now get back to your job.'

So come all you colliers, take heed what I say,
Don't believe Lord Robens when he says he'll give fair pay.
He'll tell you to work and make the output rise;
But you'll get pie in the sky instead of a pound-a-week rise.

Written in response to the Tory press's smear campaign against the miners during
their successful wages struggle in 1974.

Pat Cooksey is a semi-professional songwriter and performer currently working at
Rolls Royce in Coventry. In recent years he has built a sizeable following in the local
folk clubs and Sunday lunchtime 'free and easys'. Anyone wishing to book Pat for a
social should write to him c/o 329 Middlemarch Road, Coventry.

Pat Cooksey

UNDERGROUND ARISTOCRATS

Oh I am a jovial miner and I'm living like a lord;
Since we've received the benefits of our new pay award.
We're underground aristocrats, the envy of the land,
And with all our pay improvements won't our lives be very grand.
Now we've climbed the social ladder, we're as happy as can be.
The wife's just started boiling tripe in Beaujolais for tea,
We've Persian carpets in the hall of our ten-bedroomed house,
And I go to work each morning with me lunchbox full of grouse.
Chorus;
    Oh, we are the jovial miners, we're the lads who haul the power,
    We're digging out the nation's coal for thirty bob an hour.
    The Tories stopped our wages claim, they said it was a joke,
    But we got our money and got rid of the Tories at a stroke.

To keep up one's appearances can sometimes be a task,
But I've got a million sequins on me lunchbox and me flask.
To take me to the pit at half past eight the Rolls Royce calls;
And Norman Hartnell's coming round to fit me overalls.
With me Mary Quant style helmet and me fibre optic lamp,
And Apollo spacecraft underpants to keep me from the damp.
I see the people stop and stare as I walk down the street;
For I am a jovial miner, one of Britain's new élite.
Chorus;

Now change has happened overnight in our community;
They've built a Spanish bistro where the chip shop used to be.
To help the miners spend their pay they've opened gaming clubs,
And Frank Sinatra sings at weekends down our local pub.
Me money's banked in Switzerland, it's altogether grand;
Me Lamborgini whippets are the fastest in the land.
We open social functions, we're on everybody's lips,
And Barnsley High Street's full of topless starlets eating chips.
Chorus;

Written in 1892 at the time of a miner's strike in the North East.

Born in Shotley Bridge, Co. Durham, in 1848, Tommy Armstrong was down the pits by 1857. In the 1860s, he took part in the *soirées* put on in village institutes, to which came the Tyneside concert hall stars of the day. By the 1870s, he was running his own concert parties, but he still kept close to the pit-village culture — so close, that in the great struggles of the 1890s he was appointed bard to the leader of the miners' union. Tommy died in 1920, aged 72.

The original song has been toned down and softened by a long line of editors. Politically, the least bad recorded version is to be found on The High Level Ranters, *The Bonnie Pit Laddie* (Topic Records, 1975, 12TS 271/2). Further songs by Armstrong are to be found in *Tommy Armstrong Sings* (Frank Graham, Newcastle 1971), which also contains a biographical sketch of Armstrong by Tom Gilfellon; and in *Tommy Armstrong of Tyneside* LP (Topic Records, 1965, 12T 122), a selection of edited versions.

Tommy Armstrong

THE DURHAM STRIKE

In our Durham County, I am sorry for to say
That hunger and starvation is increasing every day;
For the want of food and coals, we know not what to do,
But with your kind assistance, we will stand the struggle through.
I need not state the reason why we have been brought so low;
The masters have behaved unkind, which everyone will know.
Because we won't lie down and let them treat us as they like,
To punish us they've stopped their pits and caused the present strike.
Chorus;

    May every Durham colliery owner that is in the fault
    Receive nine lashes with the rod, and then be rubbed with salt.
    May his back end be thick with boils, so that he cannot sit,
    And never burst until the wheels go round at every pit.

The pulley wheels have ceased to move which went so swift around.
The horses and the ponies too are brought from underground.
Our work is taken from us now, they care not if we die,
For they can eat the best of food and drink the best when dry.
The miner and his partner too, each morning have to roam
To seek for bread to feed the little hungry ones at home;
The flour barrel is empty now, their true and faithful friend,
Which makes the thousands wish today the strike was at an end.

We have done our very best as honest working men,
To let the pits commence again we've offered to them 'ten'*;
The offer they will not accept, they firmly do demand
Thirteen and a half per cent, or let their collieries stand.
Let them stand, or let them lie, to do with them as they choose;
To give them thirteen and a half, we ever shall refuse.
They're always willing to receive, but not inclined to give,
Very soon they won't allow a working man to live.

With tyranny and capital they never seem content,
Unless they are endeavouring to take from us per cent;
If it was due what they request, we willingly would grant;
We know it's not, therefore we cannot give them what they want.
The miners of Northumberland we shall for ever praise,
For being so kind in helping us those tyrannising days;
We thank the other counties too, that have been doing the same,
For every man who reads will know that we are not to blame.

*the men offered to accept a 10 per cent wage cut.

70

Parody of the famous American folk song. It was written by Joe Hill at the time of a famous strike on the Southern Pacific in 1911. For notes on Joe Hill see page 55.

Casey Jones can be heard on *The Original Talking Union* LP by the Almanac Singers (Folkways Records, FH 5285).

Joe Hill

CASEY JONES

The workers on the S.P. line to strike sent out a call;
But Casey Jones, the engineer, he wouldn't strike at all.
His boiler it was leaking, and its driver on the bum,
And his engine and its bearings, they were all out of plumb.
  Casey Jones kept his junk pile running;
  Casey Jones was working double time;
  Casey Jones got a wooden medal;
  For being good and faithful on the S.P. line.

The workers said to Casey; 'Won't you help us win this strike?'
But Casey said; 'Let me alone, you'd better take a hike.'
Then Casey's wheezy engine ran right off the worn-out track,
And Casey hit the river with an awful crack.
  Casey Jones hit the river bottom;
  Casey Jones broke his blooming spine;
  Casey Jones was an Angeleno,
  He took a trip to heaven on the S.P. Line.

When Casey Jones got up to heaven to the Pearly Gate,
He said; 'I'm Casey Jones, the guy that pulled the S.P. freight.'
'You're just the man,' said Peter, 'our musicians went on strike;
You can get a job a-scabbing anytime you like.'
  Casey Jones got a job in heaven;
  Casey Jones was doing mighty fine;
  Casey Jones went scabbing on the angels,
  Just like he did to workers on the S.P. line.

The angels got together and they said it wasn't fair
For Casey Jones to go around scabbing everywhere.
The Angel Union No. 23 they sure were there
And they promptly fired Casey down the Golden Stair
  Casey Jones went to hell a-flying;
  'Casey Jones,' the Devil said, 'Oh fine;
  Casey Jones, get busy shoveling sulphur —
  That's what you get for scabbing on the S.P. line.'

Written by Ralph Chaplin on 17 January 1915, while 'lying on the rug in his living room'. The idea 'had come to him earlier while he was in West Virginia helping the coal miners in the great Kanawha Valley strike'. Chaplin 'wanted a song to be full of revolutionary fervour and to have a chorus that was singing and defiant.' (From Fowke and Glazer, *Songs of Work and Protest*, New York, Dover 1973).

Ralph Chaplin was born in 1887 and joined the IWW in 1913. He was an active organiser, journalist, poet and cartoonist, jailed for twenty years at the Chicago IWW trials in 1918. Released in 1923 Chaplin continued to write for the movement in the twenties.

Industrial Workers of the World or Wobblies (so called, it is said, because a Chinese member described himself as 'I Wobble Wobble') was founded in Chicago in 1905 to unite all workers, skilled and unskilled, men and women, black and white into One Big Union.

More than any revolutionary movement before or since, the IWW brought into the struggle a sense of humour, a sense of poetry and song. Most of their songs were written to traditional or popular tunes; partly because they were not themselves musicians but — more important — as sardonic parodies. The IWW songs published in this collection, along with many more, can be found in the 34th edition of the *IWW Songbook*, available from 6 Coniston Ave, Oldham, Greater Manchester and in *Rebel Voices; An IWW Anthology*, edited by Joyce Kornbluh, Ann Arbor Paperbacks. A recorded version is on *The Original Talking Union* LP by the Almanac Singers (Folkways Records, FH 5285).

Ralph Chaplin

SOLIDARITY FOREVER

When the Union's inspiration through the workers' blood shall run,
There can be no power greater anywhere beneath the sun.
Yet what force on earth is weaker than the feeble strength of one?
But the Union makes us strong.

Solidarity forever
Solidarity forever
Solidarity forever
For the Union makes us strong.

Is there aught we hold in common with the greedy parasite?
Who would lash us into serfdom and would crush us with his might?
Is there anything left to us but to organise and fight?
For the Union makes us strong.
Chorus;

It is we who ploughed the prairies, built the cities where they trade;
Dug the mines and built the workshops; endless miles of railroad laid.
Now we stand outcast and starving, 'midst the wonders we have made;
But the Union makes us strong.
Chorus;

All the world that's owned by idle drones is ours and ours alone.
We have laid the wide foundations; built it skyward stone by stone.
It is ours, not to slave in, but to master and to own,
While the Union makes us strong.
Chorus;

They have taken untold millions that they never toiled to earn,
But without our brain and muscle not a single wheel can turn.
We can break their haughty power, gain our freedom when we learn
That the Union makes us strong.
Chorus;

In our hands is placed a power greater than their hoarded gold;
Greater than the might of armies, magnified a thousand-fold.
We can break their haughty power; gain our freedom when we learn
For the Union makes us strong.
Chorus;

72

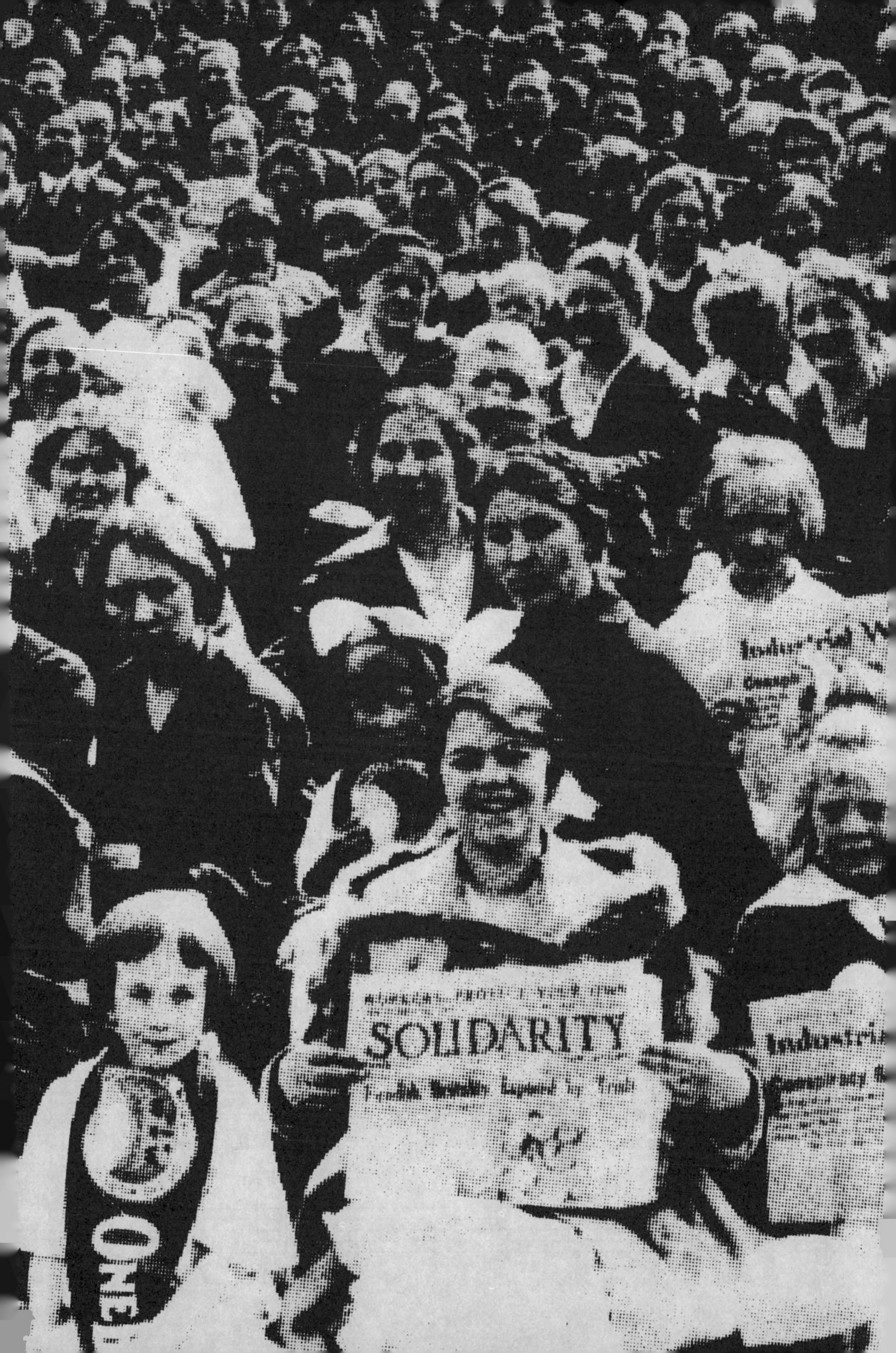
SOLIDARITY
ONE

THE INTERNATIONAL

Words: Eugene Pottier Music: Pierre Deguyter
Translator unknown

A- rise ye starv'-lings from your slum- bers A-rise ye crim-in-als of want, For reas-on in re-volt now thun-ders and at last ends the age of cant. Now a-way with all your sup-er-stit- ions, ser-vi- le ma-sses a- rise a-rise! we'll change forth-with the old con-dit- ions and spurn the dust to win the prize, Then — com- rades come rall- y and the last fight let us face, the Int- er- na- tion- al e un-

ites the hum- an race, Then com- rades come

rall- y and the last fight let us face, the

Int- er- na- tion- al- e u- nites the hum- an race.

We peasants, artisans and others;
Enrolled among the sons of toil.
Let's claim the earth henceforth for brothers,
Drive the indolent from the soil.
On our flesh too long has fed the raven;
We've too long been the vulture's prey.
But now, farewell the spirit craven,
The dawn brings in a brighter day.
Chorus;

No saviour from on high delivers;
No trust have we in prince or peer.
Our own right hand the chains must shiver;
Chains of hatred, of greed and fear.
Ere the thieves will out with their booty
And to all give a happier lot.
Each at his forge must do his duty
And strike the iron while it's hot.
Chorus;

THE RED FLAG

Words: Jim Connell Music: 'The White Cockade'

The peop-les' flag is deep-est red, It
shrouded oft our mart-yr'd dead, And 'ere their limbs grew
stiff and cold, Their hearts' blood dyed it's ev'ry fold. Then
raise the scar-let stan-dard high! Be-
neath its folds we'll live or die, Tho' cow-ards flinch and
trai-tors sneer, we'll keep the red flag fly-ing here.

Look 'round, the Frenchman loves its blaze,
The sturdy German chants its praise;
In Moscow's vaults its hymns are sung,
Chicago swells the surging throng.
Chorus;

It waved above our infant might
When all ahead seemed dark as night;
It witnessed many a deed and vow,
We must not change its colour now.
Chorus;

It well recalls the triumphs past;
It gives the hope of peace at last —

The banner bright, the symbol plain
Of human right and human gain.
Chorus;

It suits today the meek and base,
Whose minds are fixed on pelf and place,
To cringe beneath the rich man's frown,
And haul that sacred emblem down.
Chorus;

With heads uncovered swear we all
To bare it onward till we fall.
Come dungeons dark or gallows grim,
This song shall be our parting hymn.
Chorus;

BANDIERA ROSSA

With Spirit

A-rise you work-ers , fling to the breez- es   The scar- let

ban - ner,   the scar-let ban - ner A - rise, you work- ers, fling to the

breez- es The scar-let ban- ner tri- um -phant- ly   Wave scar-let ban-ner tri-

um- phant- ly,   Wave scar- let ban- ner tri- umph-ant- ly, Wave scar-let ban-ner tri-

um- phant- ly,   For — comm-un-is- im   and   lib- er   ty.

Arise you workers, your chains of slavery
Will vanish under the scarlet banner.
Come rally round it, come show your bravery;
The scarlet banner, triumphantly.
   Wave scarlet banners triumphantly
   Wave scarlet banners triumphantly
   Wave scarlet banners triumphantly.
   For communism and liberty.

VIVA LA QUINCE BRIGADA

Anon.

With sharp rhythm

Vi- va la Quin- ce Bri- ga- da, Rhum-ba-la, Rhum-ba-la, Rhum-ba- la

Vi- va la Quin- ce Bri- ga- da, Rhum-ba-la, Rhum-ba-la, Rhum-ba- la

REFRAIN

Que se-ha cu- bier- ta de glo- ri- a, Ay Man- u-

el- a, Ay Man- u- el- a -el -a

Luchamos contra los Morros,
Rhum-ba-la, rhum-ba-la, rhum-ba-la.
Mercenairos y fascistas,
Rhum-ba-la, rhum-ba-la, rhum-ba-la.

Soloex nuestro deseo,
Rhum-ba-la, rhum-ba-la, rhum-ba-la.
Acabar con el fascismo,
Rhum-ba-la, rhum-ba-la, rhum-ba-la.

En el frente de Jarama,
Rhum-ba-la, rhum-ba-la, rhum-ba-la.
No tenemos ni aviones,
Rhum-ba-la, rhum-ba-la, rhum-ba-la.
Ni tankes, ni canones,
Ay Manuela, ay Manuela.

Ya Salimos de Espana,
Rhum-ba-la, rhum-ba-la, rhum-ba-la.
Por Luchar en otras frontes,
Rhum-ba-la, rhum-ba-la, rhum-ba-la.

THE WORLD TURNED UPSIDE DOWN

Words and music: Leon Rosselson

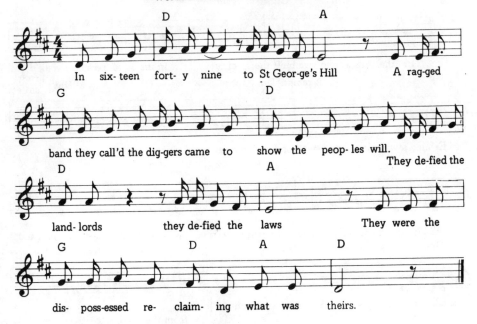

In six-teen fort-y nine to St Geor-ge's Hill A rag-ged band they call'd the dig-gers came to show the peop-les will. They de-fied the land-lords they de-fied the laws They were the dis-poss-essed re-claim-ing what was theirs.

We come in peace, they said, to dig and sow.
We come to work the land in common and to make the waste ground grow
This earth divided, we will make whole
So it will be a common treasury for all.

The sin of property we do disdain.
No man has any right to buy and sell the earth for private gain.
By theft and murder they took the land
Now everywhere the walls spring up at their command.

They make the laws to chain us well.
The clergy dazzle us with heaven or they damn us into hell.
We will not worship the God they serve
The God of greed who feeds the rich while poor men starve.

We work, we eat together, we need no swords.
We will not bow to masters or pay rent to the lords.
We are free men, though we are poor,
You Diggers all stand up for Glory, stand up now.

From the men of property the orders came.
They sent the hired men and troopers to wipe out the Diggers' claim.
Tear down their cottages, destroy their corn.
They were dispersed — only the vision lingers on.

You poor take courage, you rich take care.
This earth was made a common treasury for everyone to share;
All things in common, all people one
We come in peace — the orders came to cut them down.

THE BALLAD OF ACCOUNTING

Words and music: Ewan MacColl

In the morn-ing we built the ci-ty In the af-ter-noon walk'd thru it's streets

Ev-ning saw us lea-ving, we wand-er'd our days as if they would ne-ver end thru

All of us im-ag-in'd we had end-less time to spend, we hard-ly saw the cross-roads and

small a-tten-tion gave, to land-marks on the jour-ney from the cra-dle to the grave

cra-dle to the grave, cra-dle to the grave

Did you learn to dream in the morning?
Abandon dreams in the afternoon?
Wait without hope in the evening?
Did you stand there in the traces and let 'em feed you lies?
Did you trail along behind 'em wearing blinkers on your eyes?
Did you kiss the foot that kicked you? Did you thank 'em for their scorn?
Did you ask for their forgiveness for the act of being born?
ACT OF BEING BORN, ACT OF BEING BORN?

Did you alter the face of the city?
Make any change in the world you found?
Or did you observe all the warnings?
Did you read the trespass notices, did you keep off the grass?
Did you shuffle off the pavement just to let your betters pass?
Did you learn to keep your mouth shut, were you seen and never heard?
Did you learn to be obedient and jump to at a word?
AND JUMP TO AT A WORD, JUMP TO AT A WORD?

Did you ever demand any answers,
The who and the what and the reason why?
Did you ever question the set up?
Did you stand aside and let 'em **choose** while you took second best?
Did you let 'em skim the cream off and then give to you the rest?
Did you settle for the shoddy and did you think it right?
To let 'em rob you right and left and never make a fight?
NEVER MAKE A FIGHT, NEVER MAKE A FIGHT?

What did you learn in the morning?
How much did you know in the afternoon?
Were you content in the evening?
Did they teach you how to question when you were at school?
Did the factory help you grow, were you the maker or the tool?
Did the place where you were living enrich your life, and then —
Did you reach some understanding of all your fellow men?
ALL YOUR FELLOW MEN, ALL YOUR FELLOW MEN?

THE OLD MAN'S SONG

Words: Ian Campbell Music: Traditional

At the turn-ing of the cen-tur-y I was a boy of five Me

fath-er went to fight the Boers and ne-ver came back a-live Me

moth-er was left to bring us up, no char-it-y she'd seek So she

washed and scrubbed & scraped a-long on sev-en and six a week.

When I was twelve I left the school and went to find a job,
With growing kids me ma was glad of the extra couple of bob.
I'm sure that better schooling would have stood me in good stead,
But you can't afford refinements when you're struggling for your bread.

And when the great war came along I didn't hesitate,
I took the royal shilling and went off to do me bit.
I lived on mud and tears and blood, three years or thereabouts,
Then I copped some gas in Flanders and got invalided out.

Well when the war was over and we'd settled with the Hun,
We got back into civvies and we thought the fighting done,
We'd won the right to live in peace, but we didn't have such luck,
For soon we found we had to fight for the right to go to work.

In '26 the General Strike found me out on the streets,
Though I'd a wife a' kids by then and their needs I had to meet,
For a brave new world was coming, and the brotherhood of man,
But when the strike was over we were back where we began.

I struggled through the 'thirties, out of work now and again,
I saw the blackshirts marching, and the things they did in Spain,
So I reared me children decent, and I taught them wrong from right,
But Hitler was the lad who came along and taught them how to fight.

My daughter was a landgirl, she got married to a Yank,
And they gave me son a gong for stopping one of Rommel's tanks.
He was wounded just before the end, and convalesced in Rome,
He married an Eyetie nurse and never bothered to come home.

My daughter writes me once a month, a cheerful little note,
About their colour telly and the other things they've got,
She's got a son, a likely lad, he's nearly twenty one,
And she tells me now they've called him up to fight in Vietnam.

We're living on the pension now, it doesn't go too far,
Not much to show for a life that seems like one long bloody war,
When you think of all the wasted lives it makes you want to cry,
I'm not sure how to change things, but by Christ we'll have a try.

MRS McGRATH

Music: Traditional

'Oh Mr-s Mc-Grath', the ser- geant said, 'Would you like to make a sol-dier out of your son, Ted, With a scar- let coat and a big cocked hat? Now,

82

With your too-ri-raa, fol-the-did-le-aa, Too-ri-oo-ri-oo-ri-aa, With your too-ri-aa fol-the-did-le-aa. Too-ri-oo-ri-oo-ri-aa.

So Mrs McGrath lived on the sea-shore,
For the space of seven long years or more,
Till she saw a big ship sailing into the bay,
'Here's my son, Ted, wisha, clear the way.'
Chorus;

'Oh, Captain dear, where have you been?
Have you been sailing on the Mediterreen?
Or have ye any tidings of my son Ted,
Is the poor boy living, or is he dead?'
Chorus;

Then up comes Ted without any legs,
And in their place he has two wooden pegs,
She kissed him a dozen times or two,
Saying, 'Holy Moses, 'tisn't you.'
Chorus;

'Oh then were ye drunk, or were ye blind,
That ye left ye two fine legs behind?
Or was it walking upon the sea
Wore ye two fine legs from the knees away?'
Chorus;

'Oh I wasn't drunk, and I wasn't blind
But I left my two fine legs behind.
For a cannon ball on the fifth of May
Took my two fine legs from the knees away.'
Chorus;

'Oh then, Teddy me boy!' the widow cried,
'Ye two fine legs were ye mammy's pride.
Them stumps of a tree wouldn't do at all,
Why didn't ye run from the big cannon ball?'
Chorus;

'All foreign wars I do proclaim
Between Don John and the King of Spain.
And by herrins I'll make them rue the time
That they swept the legs from a child of mine.'
Chorus;

'Oh then, if I had you back again,
I'd never let you go to fight the King of Spain.
For I'd rather my Ted as he used to be
Than the King of France and his whole Navee.'
Chorus;

BROWNED OFF

Words and music: Ewan MacColl

I used to be a civ-vy, chum, as de-cent as can be . I used to think a work-ing lad had a man's right to be free . And then one day they made a lous-y sold-ier out of me , And told me I had got to save de-moc-ra-cy , Oh I was brown'd off, brown'd off, brown'd off as can be , Brown'd off, Brown'd off, an eas-y mark that's me , but when this war is ov-er and a-gain I am — free , There'll be no more trips a-round the world for me .

They stuck me in a convict's suit, they made me cut me hair.
They took me civvy shoes away, they gave me another pair.
Instead of grub they gave me slush and plenty of fresh air
And this was all to help to save democracy.
Chorus;

Now every day I'm on parade long before the dawn.
And every day I curse the day that I was born.
For I am just a browned off soldier, anyone can see;
They browned me off to help to save democracy.
Chorus;

The colonel kicks the major, then the major has to go,
He kicks the poor old captain who then kicks the NCO.
And as the kicks get harder the poor private, you can see,
Gets kicked to ruddy hell to save democracy.
Chorus;

WILLIAM BROWN

Words: Arthur Hagg Music: Traditional

A nice young man was Will- iam Brown, He work'd for a wage in a

York- shire town, He turn'd a wheel from left to right, from

C7   F   CHORUS F
eight at morn' till six at night. Now keep that wheel a'

C   C7   F
turn- ing   Keep that wheel a'- turn - ing

F   B   C7   F
Keep that wheel a' turn- ing,   and do a litt-le more each day

The boss one day to William came.
'Look here', he said, 'Young what's your name.
We're far from pleased with what you do;
So hurry that wheel or out you go!'
    Now keep that wheel a turning
    Keep that wheel a turning
    Keep that wheel a turning
    And do a little more each day.

So William turned and he made her run
Three times round in the place of one.
He turned so hard he was quickly made
The Lord High Turner of his trade.
    Now keep that wheel a turning
    Keep that wheel a turning
    Keep that wheel a turning
    And do a little more each day.

His fame spread wide o'er hill and dale.
His face appeared in the Daily Mail.
Cheap coach trips were organised
All to gaze at the lad's blue eyes.
    Now keep that wheel a turning
    Keep that wheel a turning
    Keep that wheel a turning
    And do a little more each day.

Still William turned with a saintly smile;
The goods he made grew such a pile.
They filled his room and the room next door
And overflowed to the basement floor.
    Now keep that wheel a turning
    Keep that wheel a turning
    Keep that wheel a turning
    And do a little more each day.

But sad the sequel now to tell;
With profits raised the boss could sell
To take-over group from London town.
The first redundant case was Brown!
Chorus;
    Now he's in the queue a' waiting,
    He's in the queue a' waiting,
    He's in the queue a' waiting,
    And he gets a little thinner each day.

Now workers don't be such a clown,
But take a tip from William Brown.
If you work too hard you'll surely be
Wiser but poorer same as he.
Chorus;
    For he's in the queue a' waiting,
    He's in the queue a' waiting,
    He's in the queue a' waiting
    And he gets a little thinner each day.

UNION MAID

Words and music: Woody Guthrie

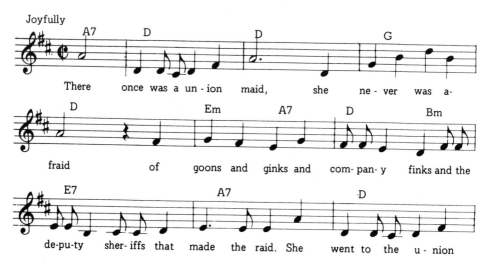

Joyfully

There once was a un-ion maid, she ne-ver was a-fraid of goons and ginks and com-pan-y finks and the de-pu-ty sher-iffs that made the raid. She went to the u-nion

hall when a meet-ing it was called And when the com-p'ny
boys came 'round she al - ways stood her ground. Oh, you
can't scare me I'm stick-ing to the un- ion I'm sticking to the
un - ion I'm stick-in' to the un- ion Oh', you
can't scare me, I'm stick-in' to the un- ion I'm stick-in' to the
un- ion till the day I die

This union maid was wise to the tricks of the company spies;
She never got fooled by a company stool, she'd always organise the guys.
She'd always get her way when she struck for higher pay;
She'd show her card to the company guard and this is what she'd say;
Chorus;

You gals who want to be free just take a little tip from me:
Get you a man who's a union man and join the Ladies' Auxiliary;
Married life ain't hard when you've got a union card,
A union man has a happy life when he's got a union wife.

A woman's struggle is hard, even with a union card;
She's got to stand on her own two feet and not be a servant of a male élite.
It's time to take a stand, keep working hand in hand,
There is a job that's got to be done, and a fight that's got to be won.
Chorus;

PALACES OF GOLD

Words and music: Leon Rosselson

If the sons of com-pa-ny di- rec- tors, And jud- ges' pri- vate dau-gh-ters . Had to go to school in a slum school, dump'd by some jo- ker in a damp back all- ey, Had to herd in - to class - rooms cramped with wor- ry, with a view on to slag - heaps and stag- nant pools, Had to file through cor- ri- dors grey with age, And play in a crack - pot con- crete cage But - tons would be pressed Rules would be

bro - ken　　　strings would be pulled

And ma - gic words spo - ken　　　In -

vi - si - ble fin - gers　would mould　Pa - la - ces of

gold　　　．　gold

If prime ministers and advertising executives,
Royal personages and bank managers' wives
Had to live out their lives in dank rooms,
Blinded by smoke and the foul air of sewers.
Rot on the walls and rats in the cellars,
In rows of dumb houses like mouldering tombs.
Had to bring up their children and watch them grow
In a wasteland of dead streets where nothing will grow.

　Buttons would be pressed,
　Rules would be broken.
　Strings would be pulled
　And magic words spoken
　Invisible fingers would mould
　Palaces of gold.

I'm not suggesting any sort of plot,
Everyone knows there's not,
But you unborn millions might like to be warned
That if you don't want to be buried alive by slagheaps,
Pitfalls and damp walls and rat traps and dead streets,
Arrange to be democratically born
The son of a company director
Or a judge's private daughter.

　Buttons would be pressed,
　Rules would be broken.
　Strings would be pulled
　And magic words spoken.
　Invisible fingers would mould
　Palaces of gold.

STRANGE FRUIT

Words: Lewis Allan Music: arranged by Billie Holiday

THE POUND-A-WEEK RISE

Words and music: Ed Pickford

Come all ye col - liers who work down the mine, From
Scot - land to South - wich from Tees - dale to Tyne, I'll
sing you the song of the pound a week rise, And the
men who were fool'd by the gov - ern - ment lies, so its
down you go, down be - low, Jack! Where you
ne - ver see the skies, And you're work - ing in a
dun - geon For your pound - a - week rise.
Oh here is a strange and bi - tter crop - .

In nineteen and sixty, not three years ago,
The mine-workers' leaders to Lord Robens did go,
Saying, 'We work very hard, every day we risk our lives,
And we ask you, here and now, for a pound-a-week rise.'
Chorus;

Then up spoke Lord Robens and made this decree;
'When the output rises, then with you I will agree
To raise up your wages and give to you fair pay,
For I was once a miner and worked hard in my day.'
Chorus;

The miners they went home and they worked hard and well;
And their lungs filled with coal-dust in the bosom of Hell,
And the output rose by fifteen, eighteen per cent and more,
And when two years had passed and gone, it rose above a score.
Chorus;

So the mine-workers' leaders went to get their hard-won prize,
And to ask Lord Robens for the pound-a-week rise.
But Robens wouldn't give a pound, he wouldn't give ten bob,
He gave them seven and six and said, 'Now get back to your job.'

So come all you colliers, take heed what I say,
Don't believe Lord Robens when he says he'll give fair pay.
He'll tell you to work and make the output rise;
But you'll get pie in the sky instead of a pound-a-week rise.

MOTOR TRADE WORKERS

Words: Don Perrygrove Music: Traditional

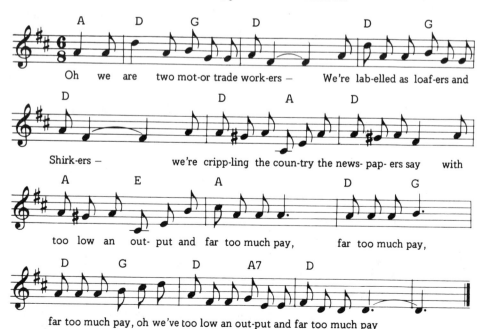

Oh we are two mot-or trade work-ers — We're lab-elled as loaf-ers and
Shirk-ers — we're cripp-ling the coun-try the news-pap-ers say with
too low an out-put and far too much pay, far too much pay,
far too much pay, oh we've too low an out-put and far too much pay

Each morning we leave around seven,
And drive to our mechanised heaven.
We make cans of tea, have a lark and a crack ,
Till the half-seven bell rings and off goes the track.
Off goes the track,
Off goes the track,
Till the half-seven bell rings and off goes the track.

Our track is a steel over-seer,
We pray he'll break down, but no fe-ar.
For his vital organs are switches and nobs;
And he has us poor working lads sweating great cobs,
Sweating great cobs,
Sweating great cobs,
And he has us poor working lads sweating great cobs.

We're pressing and turning and milling,
We're finishing and turning and drilling.
We paint a wet flat, and limit and bore,
While the foreman walks 'round like a Varna Road whore,
Varna Road whore,
Varna Road whore,
While the foreman walks 'round like a Varna Road whore.

The Big Banker who's running our nation,
Claims we are the cause of stagnation.
He sits at his desk on his fat pin-stripped arse,
While we do the donkey work, he counts the brass.
He counts the brass,
He counts the brass,
While we do the donkey work, he counts the brass.

Our trade fluctuates with the season,
That's mainly the cause and the reason;
We organise now and go in with both feet,
For tomorrow we may well be walking the streets,
Walking the streets,
Walking the streets,
For tomorrow we may well be walking the streets.

Investors and financial backers,
Are greedily counting the ackers;
Ten guineas an ounce for a working man's sweat,
Then the bastards begrudge us the wages we get.
Wages we get,
Wages we get,
Then the bastards begrudge us the wages we get.

So a word to you wealthy fat Tories
Who dream up those newspaper stories.
If it's true what they say and we're in the stew;
Then we're the red peppers, the dumplings are you.
Dumplings are you,
Dumplings are you,
Then we're the red peppers, the dumplings are you.

CLOSE THE COAL-HOUSE DOOR

Words and music: Alex Glasgow

Close the coal-house door, lad   There's

blood in-   side   Blood from bro-ken hands and feet

Blood that's dried on   pit- black meat,   Blood from hearts that know no beat, —

Close the coal-house door,   lad,

There's blood in- side

Close the coal-house door, lad, there's bones inside.
Mangled, splintered piles of bones,
Buried 'neath a mile of stones,
Not a soul to hear the groans.
Close the coal-house door,lad, there's bones inside.

Close the coal-house door, lad, there's bairns inside,
Bairns that had no time to hide,
Bairns that saw the blackness slide,
Bairns beneath the mountain side.
Close the coal-house door, lad, there's bairns inside.

Close the coal-house door, lad, and stay outside.
Geordie's standin' at the dole,
And Mrs Jackson, like a fool,
Complains about the price of coal.
Close the coal-house door, lad, there's blood inside
    There's bones inside, there's bairns inside, so stay outside.

VIGILANTE MAN

Words and music: Woody Guthrie

Mixolydian

Have you seen that vi- gi- lan- te man?

Have you seen that vi- gi- lan - te man? (I've)

(Has he) Have you seen that vi- gi- lan- te

man? I've been hearing his name all o- ver the land

✳ Omit bars (11-14) in final stanza; continue from bar 15 to the end.

Well, what is a Vigilante Man?
Tell me what is a Vigilante Man?
Has he got a gun and a club in his hand?
Is that a Vigilante Man?

Rainy night, down in the engine house;
Sleeping just as still as a mouse;
Man come along and chased us out in the rain,
Was that a Vigilante Man?

Stormy days we'd pass the time away,
Sleeping in some good warm place;
Man come along and we gave him a little race.
Was that a Vigilante Man?

Preacher Casey was just a working man,
And he said, 'Unite all you working men!'
Killed him in a river, some strange man.
Was that a Vigilante Man?

Oh, why does a Vigilante Man,
Why does a Vigilante Man,
Carry that sawed-off shotgun in his hand?
Would he shoot his brother and sister down?

I rambled around from town to town,
I rambled around from town to town;
And they herded us around like
    a wild herd of cattle,
Was that the Vigilante Men?

Have you seen that Vigilante Man?
Have you seen that Vigilante Man?
I've heard his name all over the land.

STANDING AT THE DOOR

Words and music: Alex Glasgow

When me fa-ther was a lad un-em-ploy-ment was so bad, He spent best part of his life down at the dole straight from school to the lab-our queue, Rag-gy clothes and hole-y shoes, Com-bin' pit-heaps for a man-ky bag o' coal. And I'm stand-in' at the door, at the same old blood-y door, Wait-ing for the pay-out as me fath-er did be-fore. D.C.

Nowadays we've got a craze,
To follow clever Keynesian ways,
And computers measure economic growth.
We've got experts milling round,
Writing theories on the pound;
Caring little whether we can buy a loaf.
Chorus;

'Course we didn't like the freeze,
But we really tried to please;
'Cause we made the little cross that
   put them in.
Down the river we've been sold,

For a pot of cheap Swiss gold,
And we're the ones **that** suffer for their sins.
Chorus;

Baby, baby, this is true,
I'll be standin' in this queue,
Till the Tyne runs clear and plastic roses sing.
So the next time they come by,
Watch the sky for custard pie,
And tell 'em straight, it's Humperdinck for King!
Chorus;

BREAD AND ROSES

Words: James Oppenheim Music: Caroline Kohslat

As we come marching, marching in the beau-ty of the day, A mill-ion dar-kened kit-chens, a thous-and mill lofts gray, Are touch'd with all the ra-diance that a sud-den sun dis-clo-ses, For the peo-ple hear us sing-ing, 'Bread and ros-es, Bread and ros-es'.

As we come marching, marching, we battle too for men,
For they are women's children, and we mother them again.
Our lives shall not be sweated from birth until life closes;
Hearts starve as well as bodies; give us bread, but give us roses!

As we come marching, marching, unnumbered women dead
Go crying through our singing their ancient cry for bread.
Smart art and love and beauty their drudging spirits knew.
Yes, it is bread we fight for — but we fight for roses too!

As we come marching, marching, we bring the greater days.
The rising of the women means the rising of the race.
No more the drudge and idler — ten that toil where one reposes,
But a sharing of life's glories; Bread and roses! Bread and roses!

GO DOWN YOU MURDERERS

Words and music: Ewan MacColl

For the murder of his own dear wife and the killing of his own child.
The jury found him guilty and the hanging judge he smiled,
Saying, 'Go down you murderer, go down!'

Evans pleaded innocent and he swore by Him on high,
That he never killed his own dear wife nor caused his child to die
Saying, 'Go down you murderer, go down!'

So they moved him out of C block to his final *flowery dell*,
And the day and night two *screws* were there, and they never left his cell,
Saying, 'Go down you murderer, go down!'

Sometimes they played draughts with him and solo and pontoon,
To stop him brooding on the rope that was to be his doom,
Saying, 'Go down you murderer, go down!'

They brought his grub in on a tray, there were eggs and meat and ham,
And all the *snout* that he could smoke was there at his command,
Saying, 'Go down you murderer, go down!'

Evans walked in the prison yard and the screws they walked behind,
And he saw the sky above the wall but he knew no peace of mind,
Saying, 'Go down you murderer, go down!'

They came for him at eight o'clock and the chaplain read a prayer,
And then they walked him to that place where the hangman did prepare,
Saying, 'Go down you murderer, go down!'

The rope was fixed around his neck and a washer behind his ear,
And the prison bell was tolling, but Tim Evans did not hear,
Saying, 'Go down you murderer, go down!'

A thousand *lags* were cursing and a-banging on the doors,
Tim Evans did not hear them, he was deaf forevermore,
Saying, 'Go down you murderer, go down!'

They sent Tim Evans to the *drop* for a crime he didn't do,
It was Christie was the murderer and the judge and jury too,
Saying, 'Go down you murderers, go down.'

THE FIRST TIME EVER I SAW YOUR FACE

Words and music: Ewan MacColl

The first time ever I kissed your mouth,
I felt the earth move in my hand,
Like a trembling heart of a captive bird
That was there at my command, my love,
That was there at my command.

The first time ever I lay with you,
And felt your heart beat close to mine,
I thought our joy would fill the earth
And last till the end of time, my love,
And last till the end of time.

CHEMICAL WORKERS

Words and music: Ron Angel

No Chords

A Pro- cess man am I and I'm tell- ing you no lie, I

work and breathe a - mong the fumes that trail a- cross the sky, There's

thun- der all a - round me and poi - son in the air there's a

lous- y smell that smacks of hell and dust all in me hair and it's

CHORUS Em   Em   Bm   Em

Go,   boy , Go,   They'll time your ev'- ry breath and

Em Bm   Em Bm   Em Bm   Em Bm   Em

ev' - ry day you're in this place you're near-er death, But yer go !
               two days

I've worked amongst the spinners, I've breathed in the oily smoke.
I've shovelled up the gypsum that nigh on makes you choke.
I've stood knee deep in cyanide, gone sick with a caustic burn;
Been working rough and seen enough to make your stomach turn.
Chorus;

There's overtime and bonus, opportunities galore.
Young lads like the money, and they all come back for more.
But soon you're knocking on and look older than you should;
For every bob made on this job you pay with flesh and blood.
Chorus;

BATTLE HYMN OF THE NEW SOCIALIST PARTY

Words and music: Leon Rosselson

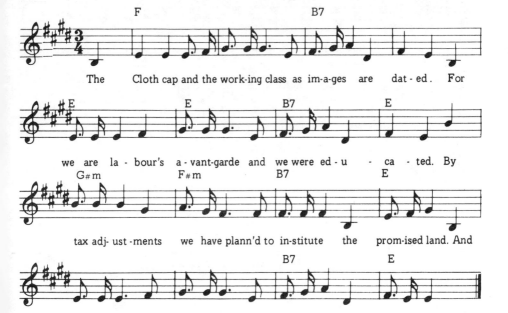

The Cloth cap and the work-ing class as im-a-ges are dat-ed. For we are la-bour's a-vant-garde and we were ed-u-ca-ted. By tax adj-ust-ments we have plann'd to in-stitute the prom-ised land. And just to show that we're sin-cere we sing the Red Flag once a year.

Firm principles and policies
Are open to objections.
And a streamlined party image is
The way to win elections.
So raise the umbrella high
The bowler hat and college tie.
We'll stand united, raise a cheer
And sing *The Red Flag* once a year.

It's one step forward, one step back
Our dance is devilish daring.
A leftward shuffle, a rightward tack,
The pause to take our bearings.
We'll reform the country, bit by bit
So nobody will notice it.
Then ever after, never fear
We'll sing *The Red Flag* once a year.

We will not cease from mental fight
Till every wrong is righted.
And all men are equal quite,
And all our leaders knighted.

For we are sure if we persist
To make the New Year's Honours List.
Then every loyal Labour Peer
Will sing *The Red Flag* once a year.

So vote for us, and not for them
We're just as true to N.A.T.O.
We'll be as calm and British when
We steer the ship of state — O.
We'll stand as firm as them*
To show we're patriotic gentlemen*
Though man to man shall brothers be;
Deterrence is our policy.

So raise the mushroom clouds on high
Within their shade we'll live — and die
Though cowards flinch and traitors sneer,
We'll sing *The Red Flag* once a year.

* These two lines sung to
'Send her victorious, Happy and glorious

I'M GONNA BE AN ENGINEER

Words and music: Peggy Seeger

Easily

When I was a lit-tle girl I wish'd I was a boy, I tagg'd a-long be-hind the gang and

wore my cord-u-roys, Ev'-ry bod-y said I on-ly did it to an-noy, But I was

gon-na be an en- gi- neer . Mom-ma told me can't you be a

la- dy? Your du-ty is to make me the mother of a pearl ,

Wait un-til you're old er, dear, and may-be you'll be glad that you're a girl

Dain-ty as a Dres-den stat-ue ; gen-tle as a Jer-sey

cow ; Smooth as silk, gives cream-y milk; Learn to coo ,

learn to moo , That's what to do to be a la-dy now ,

This Part only after verses 1, 3, 6 and 7.

When I went to school I learned to write and how to read
Some history and geography and home economy;
And typing is a skill that every girl is sure to need,
To while away the extra time until the time to breed.
And then they had the nerve to say; 'What would you like to be?'
I says, 'I'm gonna be an engineer!'
'No, you only need to learn to be a lady
The duty isn't yours, for to try and run the world.
An engineer could never have a baby,
Remember, dear, that you're a girl.'

So I become a typist and I study on the sly,
Working out the day and night so I can qualify.
And every time the boss come in, he pinched me on the thigh,
Says; 'I've never had an engineer!'
You owe it to the job to be a lady
It's the duty of the staff for to give the boss a whirl
The wages that you get are crummy, maybe
But it's all you get, 'cause you're a girl.
    She's smart! (for a woman)
    I wonder how she got that way?
    You get no choice
    You get no voice
    Just stay mum
    Pretend you're dumb
    That's how you come to be a lady today!

Then Jimmy come along and we set up a conjugation,
We were busy every night with loving recreation.
I spent my days at work so he could get his education,
And now he's an engineer!
He says; 'I know you'll always be a lady.
It's the duty of my darling to love me all her life.
Could an engineer look after or obey me?
Remember, dear, that you're my wife!

As soon as Jimmy got a job I studied hard again,
Then, busy at me turret lathe a year or so, and then,
The morning that the twins were born, Jimmy says to them,
'Kids, your mother was an engineer!'
You owe it to the kids to be a lady;
Dainty as a dishrag, faithful as a chow,
Stay at home you got to mind the baby,
Remember you're a mother now.

Every time I turn around there's something else to do,
Cook a meal or mend a sock or sweep a floor or two.
Listen in to Jimmy Young — it makes me want to spew
I was gonna be an engineer!
I really wish that I could be a lady,
I could do the lovely things that a lady's s'posed to do.
I wouldn't even mind if only they would pay me,
And I could be a person too.
    What price — for a woman?
    You can buy her for a ring of gold;

To love and obey,
(Without any pay)
You get a cook or a nurse
For better or worse
You don't need a purse when a lady is sold!

But now that times are harder, and my Jimmy's got the sack,
I went down to Vickers, they were glad to have me back,
I'm a third class citizen, my wages tell me that.
But I'm a first class engineer!
The boss he says; 'I pay you as a lady,
You only got the job 'cause I can't afford a man.
With you I keep the profits high as may be;
You're just a cheaper pair of hands!'
    You got one fault! You're a woman.
    You're not worth the equal pay.
    A bitch or a tart,
    You're nothing but heart
    Shallow and vain,
    You got no brain;
    Go down the drain like a lady today!

I listened to my mother and I joined a typing pool,
I listened to my lover and I sent him through his school.
If I listen to the boss, I'm just a bloody fool;
And an underpaid engineer!
I've been a sucker ever since I was a baby.
As a daughter, as a wife, as a mother, and a dear —
But I'll fight them as a woman, not a lady,
I'll fight them as an engineer!

JOIN THE BRITISH ARMY

Music: Irish traditional

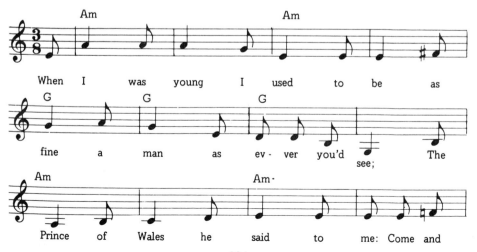

When I was young I used to be as
fine a man as ev-ver you'd see; The
Prince of Wales he said to me: Come and

104

Sarah Condon baked a cake.
'Twas all for poor old Slattery's sake.
I threw myself into the lake;
Pretending I was barmy.
   Too-ral-loo-ral-loo-ral-loo
   'Twas the only thing that I could do
   To work my ticket home to you
   And leave the British Army.

Corporal Daly's got such a drought,
Just give him a couple of jars of stout.
He'll kill the enemy with his mouth,
And save the British Army.
   Too-ral-loo-ral-loo-ral-loo
   My curses on the labour-broo
   That took my darling boy from you
   To join the British Army.

Captain Johnson went away
And his wife got in the family way.
And all the words that she could say
Was blame the British Army.
   Too-ral-loo-ral-loo-ral-loo,
   I've made my mind up what to do,
   I'll work my ticket home to you,
   And leave the British Army.

AS SOON AS THIS PUB CLOSES

Words and music: Alex Glasgow

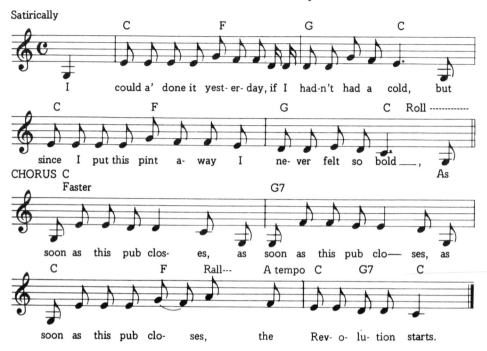

Satirically

I could a' done it yest-er-day, if I had-n't had a cold, but since I put this pint a-way I ne-ver felt so bold ___, As

CHORUS C — Faster

soon as this pub clos-es, as soon as this pub clo— ses, as soon as this pub clo- ses, the Rev-o-lu-tion starts.

I'll shoot the aristocracy
And confiscate their brass
Create a fine democracy
That's truly working class.
As soon as this pub closes
As soon as this pub closes
As soon as this pub closes
I'll raise the banner high.

I'll fight the nasty racialists
And scrap the colour bar
And all fascist dictatorships
And every commissar
As soon as this pub closes
As soon as this pub closes
As soon as this pub closes
I'll man the barricades.

So raise your glasses everyone
For everything is planned
And each and every mother's son
Will see the promised land
As soon as this pub closes
As soon as this pub closes
As soon as this pub closes
. . .I think I'm gonna be sick.

McALPINE'S FUSILIERS

Words and music: Dominic Behan

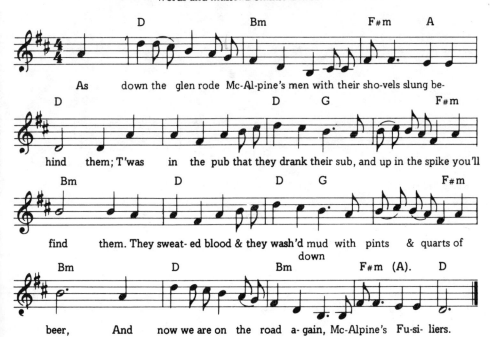

As down the glen rode Mc-Al-pine's men with their sho-vels slung be-hind them; T'was in the pub that they drank their sub, and up in the spike you'll find them. They sweat-ed blood & they wash'd mud with pints & quarts of beer, And now we are on the road a-gain, Mc-Alpine's Fu-si-liers.

I've stripped to the skin with Darkie Finn
Down upon the Isle of Grain.
With Horseface Toole I knew the rule;
No bonus if you stopped for rain.
While McAlpine's god was a well-filled hod
With your shoulders cut and seared,
And woe to he went to look for tea
With McAlpine's Fusiliers.

I mind the day when the bear O'Shea
Fell into a concrete stair.
What Horseface said when he saw him dead
Wasn't what the rich call prayers.
I'm a navvy short was the one retort
That reached unto my ears.
When the going is rough you must be tough
With McAlpine's Fusiliers.

I've worked 'till sweat has had me bet
With Russian, Czech and Pole;
On the shuttering jams upon the hydro dams,
Or down below the Thames in a hole.
I've grafted hard and I've got my cards
And many a ganger's fist across my ears.
If you pride your life don't join, by Christ,
With McAlpine's Fusiliers.

THE PREACHER AND THE SLAVE

Words: Joe Hill Music: Traditional: Sweet Bye and Bye

Long hair'd preach-ers come out ev-ry night. Try to tell you what's wrong and what's right-, But when asked about somethin' to eat; They will an-swer with voi-ces so sweet:

REFRAIN

you will eat by and by In that glo - ri -ous land above the sky. Work and pray; live on hay; You'll get pie in the sky when you die

And the starvation army they play,
And they sing and they clap and they pray.
Till they get all your coin on the drum,
Then they tell you when you're on the bum;
Chorus;

If you fight hard for children and wife —
Try to get something good in this life.
You're a sinner and bad man, they tell,
When you die you will sure go to hell.
Chorus;

Workingmen of all countries unite,
Side by side we for freedom will fight;
When the world and its wealth we have gained,
To the grafters we'll sing this refrain;
Final Chorus;
    You will eat, bye and bye;
    When you've learned how to cook and to fry.
    Chop some wood, 'twill do you good,
    And you'll eat in the sweet bye and bye.

THE BLACKLEG MINER

Music: Traditional

It's in the even-ing af-ter dark, When a
Black-leg min-er creeps te work, With his
mole-skin pants and dor-ty shirt, There
goes the black-leg min-er!

He'll take his picks and down he goes
Te hew the coal that lies below
But there's not a woman in this town row
Will look at a blackleg miner.

Now, divvent gan near the Delavel mine
Across the way they stretch a line
Te catch the throat an' break the spine
Of the dorty blackleg miner.

An' Seghill is a terrible place
They rub wet clay in a blackleg's face
An' around the heap they run a foot race
Te catch the blackleg miner.

They take ye duds an' tools as well
An' hoy them doon the pit of hell
Down ye go an' fare ye well
Ye dorty blackleg miner.

So join the union while ye may
Don't wait till yer dyin' day
'Cause that may not be far away
Ye dorty blackleg miner.

THE PEELERS AND THE GOAT

Music: Traditional

Unaccompanied

Oh the Ban-sha peel- ers went one night on du- ty at the trown-ing-o, They

met a goat up- on the road and took him for a- stroll-ing- o, With

bay'- nets fixed, they sall-ied forth and comm-an-deered the whi- zzen-o, And

then they swore out migh- ty oaths and sent him off to pri- son- o.

'Oh mercy sir,' the goat replied,
'And let me tell me story – O
Sure I'm no rogue or ribon man,
Nor croppie   Whig or Tory – O
I'm guilty not of any crime;
Of petty or high treason – O
And our tribe is wanted at this time;
For this is the ranting season – O'.

'It is in vain for to complain,
Or give your tongue such bridle – O
You're absent from your dwelling place,
Disorderly and idle – O
Your hoary locks will not prevail,
Nor your sublime oration – O
For Penal Laws will you transport
On your own information – O'

'No Penal Laws did I transgress,
By deed or combination   – O
I have no certain place of rest;
Nor home or habitation – O
But Bansha is my dwelling place,
Where I was born and bred – O
I descended from an honest race;
That's all the trade I've leaden – O'

'I will chastise your insolence
And violent behaviour – O
Well bound to Cashell   you'll be sent
Where you will gain no favour – O
The magistrates will all consent
To sign your condemnation – O
From there to Cork you will be sent
For speedy transportation – O'

'This parish and this neighbourhood
Are peaceable and tranquil – O
There's no disturbance here, thank God,
And long may it continue – so.
I don't regard your author pin,
And sign for my committal – O
My jury will be gentlemen
And grant me my acquittal – O'

'The consequence be what it will,
The peeler's power, I'll let you know,
I'll handcuff you at all events
And march you to the Bridewell   – O
And sure, you rogue, you can't deny
Before the judge or jury – O
Intimidation with your horns,
And threatening me with fury – O'

'I make no doubt that you are drunk,
With whiskey, rum or brandy — O
Or you wouldn't have such gallant spunk
To be so bald or manly — O
You readily would let me pass
If I had money handy — O
To treat you to a potcheen glass,
Oh 'tis then I'd be the dandy — O.'

HALLELUJAH I'M A BUM

Words and music: Harry McClintock

Why don't you work like o- ther men do? How in
Hell can I work when there's no work to do? Hal- le-
lu- jah, I'm a bum, Hal- le- lu- jah, bum a- gain; · Hal- le-
lu- jah give us a hand- out To re- vive us a- gain! a gain!

Oh, why don't you save
All the money you earn?
If I did not eat
I'd have money to burn.
Chorus;

Oh, I like my boss —
He's a good friend of mine;
That's why I am starving
Out in the breadline.
Chorus;

I can't buy a job
For I ain't got the dough,
So I ride in a box-car
For I'm a hobo.
Chorus;

Whenever I get
All the money I earn
The boss will be broke
And to work he must turn.
Chorus;

THE PEAT-BOG SOLDIERS

Music: Traditional

In March Rhythm

Far and wide as the eye can wan- der
Heath and bog are ev'- ry- where.
Not a bird sings out to cheer us.
Oaks are stand- ing gaunt and bare.
We are the peat- bog sol diers; We're
march- ing with our spades. To the moor

Up and down the guards are pacing;
No one, no one can go through.
Flight would mean a sure death facing,
Guns and barbed wire greet our view.
Chorus;

But for us there's no complaining,
Winter will in time be past.
One day we shall cry rejoicing,
Homeland, dear you're mine at last.
Final chorus;
    Then will the peat-bog soldiers
    March no more with their spades
    To the moor

THE MAN THAT WATERS THE WORKERS' BEER

Words and music: Paddy Ryan

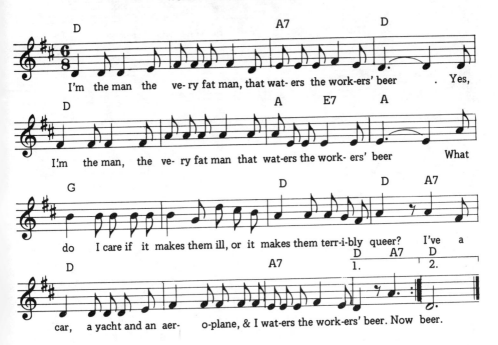

I'm the man the ve-ry fat man, that wat-ers the work-ers' beer . Yes, I'm the man, the ve-ry fat man that wat-ers the work-ers' beer What do I care if it makes them ill, or it makes them terr-i-bly queer? I've a car, a yacht and an aer-o-plane, & I wat-ers the work-ers' beer. Now beer.

Now, when I makes the workers' beer I puts in strychinine;
Some methylated sprits and a drop of paraffine.
But since a brew so terribly strong might make them terribly queer;
I reaches my hand for the water tap and I waters the workers' beer!
Chorus;

Now, a drop of good beer is good for a man who's thirsty and tired and hot,
And I sometimes has a drop for myself from a very special lot.
But a fat and healthy working class is the thing that I most fear;
So I reaches my hand for my water tap and I waters the workers' beer.
Chorus;

Now, ladies, fair, beyond compare, and be ye maid or wife.
Oh, sometimes lend a thought for me who leads a wand'ring life.
The water rates are shockingly high, and the 'meth' is shockingly dear.
And there isn't the profit there used to be in wat'ring the workers' beer!

OAKEY STRIKE EVICTIONS

Words and music: Tommy Armstrong

It wis in No-vem-ber en aw ni-vor will for-get _____, Th'

pol-is-ses en th' can-dy-men it Oak-ey's hoos-es met _____,

John-ny th' bel-min he wis thare squint-in roond e-boot _____, En he

plaic'd three men it iv'-ry hoose te torn th' pit-men oot _____, Oh

Wat wad aw dee _____, if ad th' poo-wer me-sel'? ___ Aw'd

hang th' twen-ty can-dy-men en John-ny thit car-rys th' bell _____,

Thare th' went freh hoose to hoose te put things on th' road,
But mind th' didn't hort thorsels we liften hevy loads;
Sum wid carry th' poke oot, the fender, or th' rake,
If th' lifted two it once it wis a greet mistake.
Chorus;

Sum e theese dandy-candy men wis drest up like e cloon;
Sum ad hats wivoot e flipe, en sum wivoot e croon;
Sum ad nee laps ipon thor cotes but thare wis one chep warse;
Ivory time he ad te stoop it was e laffible farse.
Chorus;

114

Thare wis one chep ad nee sleeves nor buttins ipon hees cote;
Enuther ad e bairns hippin lapt eroond his throte.
One chep wore e pair e breeks thit belang tiv e boi,
One leg wis e sort iv e tweed, th' tuthor wis cordyroi.
Chorus;

Next thare cums th' maistor's, aw think thae shud think shem
Depriven wives en familys of a comfortible yem.
But wen thae shift freh ware thae liv, aw hope thail gan te th' well
Elang we th' twenty candymen, en Johny thit carry's th' bell.
Chorus;

THE BALLAD OF JOHN MACLEAN

Words: Matt McGinn Music: arranged by Matt McGinn

March-like

'Tell me where yer gan, lad, and who yer gan to meet?' 'I'm

head-ing for the stat- ion that's in Mc- Ad- am Street. I'll

join two hun- dred thou-sand that's there to meet the train, that's

bring-ing back to Glas-cow our own dear John Mac- lean, Dom-in-

-ay _____ . Dom-in- ay _____

There was none like John Mac-lean the fight-ing Dom-in- ay _____

Tell me where's he been lad?
Why has he been there?
They've had him in the prison
For preaching in the Square.
Johnny held a finger
At all the ills he saw.
He was right side o' the people
And wrong side o' the law.
Chorus;

Johnny was a teacher
In one of Glasgow's schools.
The golden law was silence,
But Johnny broke the rules.
For a world of social justice
Young Johnny could ne wait;
He took his chalk and easel
To the men at the shipyard gate.
Chorus;

The leaders of the nation
Make money hand o'er fist;
By grinding down the people
With the fiddle and the twist.
Aided and abetted
By preacher and the press.
John called for Revolution,
And he called for nothing less.
Chorus;

The bosses and the judges
United as one man.
For Johnny was a menace
To the '14-'18 plan.
They wanted men for slaughter
On the fields of Armentières;
John called upon the people
To smash the profiteers.
Chorus;

They brought him to the courtroom
In Edinburgh town.
But still he did not cower,
He firmly held his ground
And stoutly he defended
His every word and deed;
Five years it was the sentence
In the jail of Peterheid.
Chorus;

Seven months he lingered
In prison misery.
The people roused in fury
In Glasgow and Dundee.
Lloyd George and all his cronies
Were shaken to the core.
The prison gates were open
And Johnny's free once more.
Chorus;

TURNING THE CLOCK BACK

Words and music: Alex Glasgow

My gran-ny tells me that she's seen it all be-fore, And at
nine-ty-four she's seen a thing or two _____. She's seen the

Stock - brok - ers cry-ing, and the spec- u- la- tors sigh-ing, and the

mill - ion - aires re- ly- ing on a war to pull them through _____

CHORUS

_____ . And they're turn- ing the clock back I can hear me gran- ny

say; Yes they're turn- ing the clock back and the work-ing man will

pay _____ .

My gran remembers the way it used to be
With Baldwin and MacDonald in the chair.
She fetched the soup from down the kitchen,
Heard the speeches, saw men marching,
Read how Churchill sent the troops in,
Which the papers said was fair.
Chorus;
    And they're turning the clock back
    I can hear me granny say;
    Yes they're turning the clock back
    And the working man will pay.

My granny tells me that they're at it once again;
The nobs can't get their profits quite as high.
And Tom and Dick and Harry
Have forgotten that they carry
On their shoulders all the parasites
That suck their bodies dry.
Chorus;
    And they're turning the clock back
    I can hear me granny say.
    They may call it Social Contract
    But the working man will pay.

My granny tells me that it's getting very late,
And we've got our silly heads stuck in the sand.
She says she's got a feeling
We may very soon be reeling
From the evil dealing jackboots
As the blackshirts haunt the land.
Chorus;
    And they're turning the clock back
    I can hear me granny say
    Yes they're turning the clock back
    And the working man will pay.

THE FOUR LOOM WEAVER

Music: Traditional

Aw'ma poor cot-ton way-ver as mo-ney a one knaws. Aw've nowt t'ate i' th' heawse un' aw've wore eawt my cloas. You'd hard-ly gie six-pence for all aw've on. Meh clogs ur' booath baws'n un' stock-ings aw've none. Yo'd-think it wur hard to be sent in to th'ward To— clem un' do th'best ot yo' con _____ .

Eawr parish-church pa'son's kept telling us lung.
We'st see better toimes, if aw'd but howd my tung;
Aw've howden my tung, till aw con hardly draw breoth
Aw think i my heart he meons t' clem me to deoth;
Aw knaw he lives weel, wi' backbitin' the de'il
Bur he never pick'd o'er in his loife.

Wey tooart on six week, thinkin' aich day wur th' last,
Wey tarried un' shifted, till neaw wey're quite fast;
Wey liv't upon nettles, whoile nettles were good;
Un' Wayterloo porritch wur' th' best o' us food;
Aw'm tellin yo' true, aw con foind foak enoo
Thot're livin' no better nur me.

Neaw, owd Bill o'Dan's sent bailies   one day,
Fur t' shop scoar aw'd ow'd him, 'ot aw' couldn't pay;
Bur he're just to lat, fur owd Bill o' Bent,
Had sent eit'un cart, un' ta'en goods fur t'rent.
They laft nowt bur a stool ot're seeots for two,
Un' on it sat Marget un' me.

The bailies sceawlt reawnd us os sly os a meawse,
When they seedn 'o th' things wur ta'en eawt o' the heawse;
Un' t' one says to th' tother, 'O's gone, theaw may see.'
Aw said 'Never fret lads, you're welcome ta' me;'
They made no moor ado, bur ipt up th'owd stoo',
Un' wey booath leeten swack upon th' flags .

Aw geet howd o' eawr Marget, for hoo're strucken sick,
Hoo said, hoo'd ne'er had sich a ba-g sin' hoo're wick,
The bailies sceawrt off, wi' th' owd stoo' on their back,
Un they wouldn't ha'e caret if they'd brokken her neck.
They'rn so made at own Bent, 'cos he'd ta'en goods fur rent,
Till they'rn ready to flee us alive.

Aw said to eawr Marget, as wey lien upon th' floor,
'Wey ne'er shall be lower i' this wo'ald, aw'm sure,
Fur if wey mun alter, aw'm sure wey mum mend,
Fur aw think i' my heart wey're booath at fur end,
Fur mayt wey han none, nur no looms to wayve on,
Ecod! th' looms are as well lost as fun.'

My piece wur cheeont off, un' aw took it him back;
Aw hardly durst spake, mester looked so black —
He said; 'Yo're o'erpaid last 'oime 'ot you coom.'
Aw said, 'If aw'wur, 'twui wi' wayving beawt loom;
Un i' t' moind 'ot aw'm in, aw'st ne'er pick o'er again,
For aw've wooven mysel' to th' fur end.'

So aw coom eawt o' th' wareheawse, un' laft him chew that,
When aw thowt 'ot o' things, aw're so vext that aw swat;
Fur to think aw mun warch , to keep him un' o' th' set,
O' th' days o' my loife, un' then dee i' th'r debt;
But aw'll give o'er this made, un' work wi' a spade,
Or goo un' break stone upo' th' road.

Eawr Marget declares, if hoo'd cloas to put on,
Hoo'd go up to Lunnen   to see the great mon;
Un' if things did no' awter, when theere hoo had been,
Hoo says hoo'd begin, un' feight blood up to th' e'en,
Hoo's nout agen th' King, bur hoo loikes a fair thing,
Un' hoo says hoo con tell when hoo's hurt.

THE SOCIALIST A.B.C.

Words and music: Alex Glasgow

Intro. 1.When that I was and a litt- le tin- y boy, Me,
Ending. 2.Now that I'm not and a litt- le tin- y boy, Me

Dad- dy said to me , The time has come me bo-nny bonn-y to
Dad- dy says to me , Please try to for-get the things I said es-
bairn

learn your A B C Now Dad-dy was lodge in the coal fields chairman of the Tyne And
pecially the A B C For* that
To

A B C was different From the Enid Bly-ton kind. He sang

*Coda

* 2. Dad-dy's no longer a Un- ion man and he's had to change his plea. His

alph- a-bet is diff-'rent now, since they made him a lab-our M.P.!

Verse *

A is for Al- i- en- a -tion that

made me the man that I am and

120

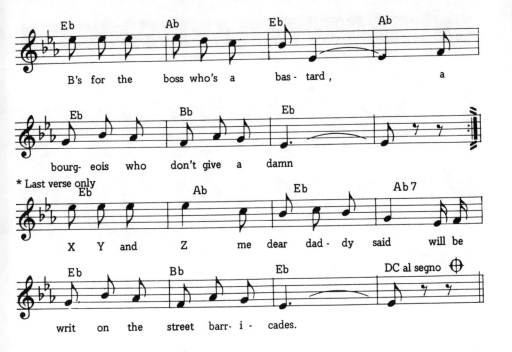

B's for the boss who's a bas-tard, a bourg-eois who don't give a damn

Last verse only

X Y and Z me dear dad-dy said will be writ on the street barr-i-cades.

C is for Capitalism, the boss's reactionary creed and D's for Dictatorship, laddie, but the best proletarian breed.
E is for Exploitation, that the workers have suffered so long;
and F is for old Ludwig Feuerbach, the first one to see it was wrong,
G is for all Gerrymanderers, like Lord Muck and Sir Whatsisname,
and H is the Hell that they'll go to, when the workers have kindled the flame.
I is for Imperialism, and America's kind is the worst,
and J is for sweet Jingoism, that the Tories all think of first.
K is for good old Keir Hardie, who fought out the working class fight
and L is for Vladimir Lenin, who showed him the Left was all right.
M is of course for Karl Marx, the daddy and the mammy of them all,
and N is for Nationalisation, without it we'd crumble and fall.
O is for Overproduction that capitalist economy brings,
and P is for all Private Property, the greatest of all of the sins.
Q is for the Quid pro quo, that we'll deal out so well and so soon,
when R for Revolution is shouted and the Red Flag becomes the top tune.
S is for sad Stalinism, that gave us all such a bad name,
and T is for Trotsky the hero, who had to take all of the blame.
U's for the Union of workers, the Union will stand to the end,
and V is for Vodka, yes, Vodka, the one drink that don't bring the bends.
W is for all Willing workers, and that's where the memory fades,
for X, Y and Z, me dear daddy said, will be written on the street barricades.

UNDERGROUND ARISTOCRATS

Words: Pat Cooksey Music: Traditional

Oh I am a jov- ial min- er and I'm
Oh we're un- der-ground ar- ist- o- crats the

liv- ing like a Lord, since we re-ceived the
en- vy of the land, and with all our pay im-

ben- e- fits of our new pay a- ward.
prove-ments won't our lives be ve- ry grand, we've

climb'd the soc- ial lad- der and we're hap- py as can be, the

wife's just start- ed boil- ing tripe in beau- jol-ais for tea, with

per- sian car- pets in the hall of our ten bed-roomed house, and I

go to work each morn- ing with me lunch- box full of grouse!

Chorus;
    Oh, we are the jovial miners, we're the lads who haul the power,
    We're digging out the nation's coal for thirty bob an hour.
    The Tories stopped our wages claim, they said it was a joke,
    But we got our money and got rid of the **Tories** at a stroke.

To keep up one's appearances can sometimes be a task,
But I've got a million sequins on me lunchbox and me flask.
To take me to the pit at half past eight the Rolls Royce calls;
And Norman Hartnell's coming round to fit me overalls.
With me Mary Quant style helmet and me fibre-optic lamp,
And Apollo spacecraft underpants to keep me from the damp.
I see the people stop and stare as I walk down the street;
For I am a jovial miner, one of Britain's new élite.
Chorus;

Now change has happened overnight in our community;
They've built a Spanish bistro where the chip shop used to be.
To help the miners spend their pay they've opened gaming clubs,
And Frank Sinatra sings at weekends down our local pub.
Me money's banked in Switzerland, it's altogether grand;
Me Lamborgini whippets are the fastest in the land.
We open social functions, we're on everybody's lips,
And Barnsley High Street's full of topless starlets eating chips.
Chorus;

THE DURHAM STRIKE

Words: Tommy Armstrong Music: Traditional

No chords

In our Dur-ham coun-ty I am sor-ry for to say, that
hung-er and starv-a-tion is in-creas-ing ev'-ry day for the
want of food and cloth-ing we know not what to do, but
with your kind a-ssist-ance we will stand the strugg-le through.

I need not state the reason why we have been brought so low;
The masters have behaved unkind, which everyone will know.
Because we won't lie down and let them treat us as they like,
To punish us they've stopped their pits and caused the present strike.

123

Chorus;

May every Durham colliery owner that is in the fault
Receive nine lashes with the rod, and then be rubbed with salt.
May his back end be thick with boils, so that he cannot sit,
And never burst until the wheels go round at every pit.

The pulley wheels have ceased to move which went so swift around.
The horses and the ponies too are brought from underground.
Our work is taken from us now, they care not if we die,
For they can eat the best of food and drink the best when dry.
The miner and his partner too, each morning have to roam
To seek for bread to feed the little hungry ones at home;
The flour barrel is empty now, their true and faithful friend,
Which makes the thousands wish today the strike was at an end.

We have done our very best as honest working men,
To let the pits commence again we've offered to them 'ten';
The offer they will not accept, they firmly do demand
Thirteen and a half per cent, or let their collieries stand.
Let them stand, or let them lie, to do with them as they choose;
To give them thirteen and a half, we ever shall refuse.
They're always willing to receive, but not inclined to give,
Very soon they won't allow a working man to live.

With tyranny and capital they never seem content,
Unless they are endeavouring to take from us per cent;
If it was due what they request, we willingly would grant;
We know it's not, therefore we cannot give them what they want.
The miners of Northumberland we shall for ever praise,
For being so kind in helping us those tyrannising days;
We thank the other counties too, that have been doing the same,
For every man who reads will know that we are not to blame.

THREE NIGHTS AND A SUNDAY DOUBLE-TIME

Words and Music: Matt McGinn

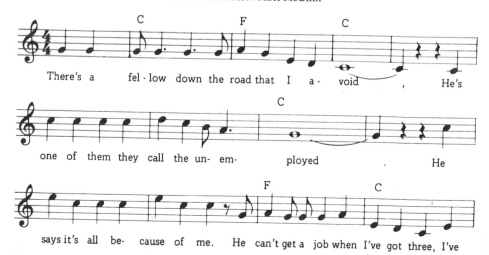

There's a fel-low down the road that I a-void, He's
one of them they call the un-em-ployed. He
says it's all be-cause of me. He can't get a job when I've got three, I've

three nights and a Sun-day dou-ble   time

CHORUS

Three   nights and a Sun- day dou- ble   time

I work all day and I work all   night, To

Hell wi' you, Jack,   I'm all right, I've   three   nights and a

Sun - day dou-ble   time

The wife came to the works the other day,
Said she, 'We've another wee one on the way.'
Says I, 'Nae wonder you can laugh —
I've no been hame for a year and a half!'
I've three nights and a Sunday double time.
Chorus;

They've gone and introduced a new machine,
There's ten men where they once had seventeen.
The machine does the work of four you see,
And I do the work of the other three,
I've three nights and a Sunday double time.
Chorus;

I've a big Post Office book it's true,
I must be worth a fiver more than you.
I saved by eating potted head —
It'll pay for the hearse when I drop dead.
I've three nights and a Sunday double time.
Chorus;

I never miss the pub on a Friday night,
And there you'll always find me gay and bright.
You'll see me down at the old Pack Horse —
I'm a weekend waiter there of course.
I've three nights and a Sunday double time.
Chorus;

Some'll head for heaven when they die,
To find a Dunlopillo in the sky.
But I'll be going to the other place,
For an idle life I couldn't face.
I've three nights and a Sunday double time.
Chorus;

CASEY JONES

Words: Joe Hill Music: Traditional

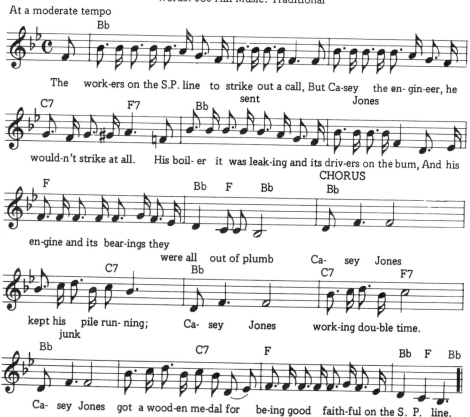

At a moderate tempo

The work-ers on the S.P. line to strike sent out a call, But Ca-sey Jones the en-gin-eer, he would-n't strike at all. His boil-er it was leak-ing and its driv-ers on the bum, And his en-gine and its bear-ings they were all out of plumb Ca-sey Jones kept his junk pile run-ning; Ca-sey Jones work-ing dou-ble time. Ca-sey Jones got a wood-en me-dal for be-ing good and faith-ful on the S. P. line.

CHORUS

The workers said to Casey; 'Won't you help us win this strike?'
But Casey said; 'Let me alone, you'd better take a hike.'
Then Casey's wheezy engine ran right off the worn-out track,
And Casey hit the river with an awful crack.
    Casey Jones hit the river bottom;
    Casey Jones broke his blooming spine;
    Casey Jones was an Angeleno,
    He took a trip to heaven on the S.P. Line.

When Casey Jones got up to heaven to the Pearly Gate,
He said; 'I'm Casey Jones, the guy that pulled the S.P. freight.'
'You're just the man,' said Peter, 'our musicians went on strike;
You can get a job a-scabbing anytime you like.'
    Casey Jones got a job in heaven;
    Casey Jones was doing mighty fine;
    Casey Jones went scabbing on the angels,
    Just like he did to workers on the S.P. line.

The angels got together and they said it wasn't fair
For Casey Jones to go around scabbing everywhere.
The Angel Union No. 23 they sure were there
And they promptly fired Casey down the Golden Stair
    Casey Jones went to hell a-flying;
    'Casey Jones,' the Devil said, 'Oh fine;
    Casey Jones, get busy shoveling sulphur —
    That's what you get for scabbing on the S.P. line.'

SOLIDARITY FOREVER

Words: Ralph Chaplin Music: to tune of 'John Brown's Body'

When the un-ion's in-spir-a- tion thru' the worker's blood shall run, There can
be no pow- er great- er an- y - where be-neath the sun; yet what
force on earth is weak- er than the fee- ble strength of one, But the
un- ion makes us strong
So- li- dar- it- y for ev- er
So- li- da- ri- ty for ev- er

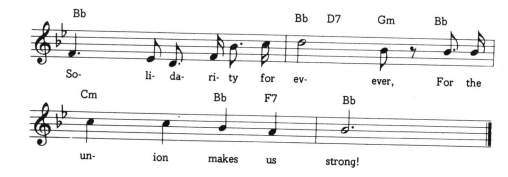

So- li- da- ri- ty for ev- ever, For the un- ion makes us strong!

Is there aught we hold in common with the greedy parasite?
Who would lash us into serfdom and would crush us with his might?
Is there anything left to us but to organise and fight?
For the Union makes us strong.
Chorus;

It is we who ploughed the prairies, built the cities where they trade;
Dug the mines and built the workshops; endless miles of railroad laid.
Now we stand outcast and starving, 'midst the wonders we have made;
But the Union makes us strong.
Chorus;

All the world that's owned by idle drones is ours and ours alone.
We have laid the wide foundations; built it skyward stone by stone.
It is ours, not to slave in, but to master and to own,
While the Union makes us strong.
Chorus;

They have taken untold millions that they never toiled to earn,
But without our brain and muscle not a single wheel can turn.
We can break their haughty power, gain our freedom when we learn
That the Union makes us strong.
Chorus;

In our hands is placed a power greater than their hoarded gold;
Greater than the might of armies, magnified a thousand-fold.
We can break their haughty power; gain our freedom when we learn
For the Union makes us strong.
Chorus;